The
Book of ECK Parables

This book has been authored by and published under the supervision of the Living ECK Master, Sri Harold Klemp. It is the Word of ECK.

The
Book of
ECK Parables

Harold Klemp
Volume 1

ECKANKAR
Minneapolis, MN

The Book of ECK Parables, Volume 1

Copyright © 1986 ECKANKAR

Printed in U.S.A.
ISBN: 0-88155-046-9
Library of Congress Catalog Card Number: 86-082644
Compiled by Heather Hughes Calero
Edited by Joan Klemp and Anthony Moore
Illustrations by Stan Burgess
Back cover photo by Robert Huntley

Contents

Chapter Nine: INTUITION/IMAGINATION

Chapter Ten: TRUTH

Chapter Eleven: INNER AND OUTER MASTERS

Chapter Twelve: INITIATION

Introduction

Here is finally a book that makes the study of God something to enjoy. The spiritual and material forces are forever at play with each other, like two rival ball teams. When the game is over, somebody won; somebody lost.

In a series of light stories, Sri Harold Klemp, spiritual leader of thousands of ECKANKAR followers around the world, brings home to us the meaning of real spiritual living today. Is it what you think?

In ancient Egypt, for example, it was a privilege to be a temple worker, even a humble monk. "A Spiritual Fallacy" tells of the severe tests that a seeker of God might endure before being accepted into the temple. It often meant giving up all things of value, including home and family. Today it is much easier to follow the path to God, but is our satisfaction as great as it was for the Egyptian monk?

And what is the right way to pray? There is a right way—and many wrong ways. "The ECK Way to Pray" does not preach, but it points to the harm done by prayers that control others. The story shows an executive's simple way to pray.

Over ninety stories, parables, and selections give the secret ways of God in fireside English. They are from Sri Harold Klemp's talks in all parts of the world: America, Europe, Africa, Asia, and Australia.

But what has this book for you? Let's just say it is a door to a new understanding of God. Just that. No more. Whatever your religion. See if you agree.

When Soul woke up in Its first body, It was given baggage, a suitcase full of karma; and when It opened it, everything went wrong. The seeds of anger, lust, vanity, greed, and attachment had been sown.

Chapter One

Karma

1. Journey of Soul

In Soul's first human incarnation, It was given karma by the negative power, or Satan, who works under the auspices of God to provide experience. The negative power was told, "Here is Soul, a pupil. Put It in your classroom. Give It the lessons It requires in the physical world to take Its place as a Co-worker in the God Worlds."

And Kal Niranjan, known as the negative power, or Satan, said, "Fine, wonderful. I'll do my best."

When Soul woke up in Its first body, It was given baggage, a suitcase full of karma; and when It opened it, everything went wrong. It was on Its way. The seeds of anger, lust, vanity, greed, and attachment had been sown.

When someone looked at him cross-eyed, the individual punched him out or hit him with a club. Of course, that set up a chain reaction. The guy who was hit wasn't as big, so he took a club and pounded someone smaller. The man who struck first was responsible. And this kept on until the person was well on his way to accumulating more karma.

The Kal Niranjan was sitting somewhere above, pulling the strings and having a good laugh. As the negative power, he was merely doing his job to give Soul every experience in life. He would push It here, push It there, and stretch It through lifetime after lifetime until, finally, Soul started developing the eyesight to see through the clouds upon which the negative power was sitting. It got a glimpse of the Kal Niranjan. "Hey, that guy's laughing at me," Soul realized for the first time.

In the beginning of Soul's sojourn here on the physical plane, It spent a number of lives too busy looking at the ground, wondering what It was doing here and what life was all about. But gradually, after eons of pain and sorrow, joy and happiness, It became a bit more experienced. Soul's vision was raised a little bit more. Finally, It looked high enough to see Kal Niranjan sitting there. "Oh, now I see," Soul said. "This is where I have been getting my negative thoughts. This is where the five passions of the mind—anger, lust, attachment, greed, and vanity—have come from."

As Its vision expanded, Soul knew there was a way out of this world. First It saw the tricks of the negative force, and then It became aware that there was a way out. A little further up was someone else looking over the shoulder of Kal Niranjan. It was the Blue Light of ECK. It was the Mahanta, waiting.

2. Jamboree of Life

The Boy Scouts hold an annual jamboree, an event when all the troops throughout the state gather together for a campout. Of course, it is also a time for fun and middle-of-the-night tricks. One of the tricks is to sneak around after everyone is asleep and loosen the ropes from all the stakes holding up the tents. A couple of the boys sharing the same tent did just that. With precision movements, they moved noiselessly throughout the camp and set everybody's tent to collapsing. There was sudden and total confusion in the camp. Everybody was running around hollering at everybody else.

When the noise subsided, the boys who did it ran back to their tent, laughing. They thought they had done something funny, only they overlooked one little thing. If they had been really smart, they would have loosened the ropes on their own tent as well. As it was, all the tents in camp were down except theirs.

The next night was tough on them. They had to stand guard all night to keep the other fellas, who wanted to get even, away from their tent. They hadn't learned that if you are going to pull a prank, you have to make yourself look like one of the people who had the prank pulled on him, too. They overlooked the most important detail.

This is also the mistake many make in living life. They become so smart that they overlook the most important details. This is especially true of people who become very intellectual. It seems that the more intellectual one becomes, the more difficult it is to see and hear the spiritual essence of God—the Light and the Sound.

I have no objections to someone doing whatever he has to do to survive, because whatever is done is balanced out with the Law of Life. There will come a time when life requires full payment for whatever was extracted from it.

3. Candy Thieves

My daughter went to the store with some friends. They were all little characters, seven years old or so. Suddenly, she saw that they were scooping candy off the shelves and stuffing it into their pockets and shirts. Quickly she went over to them. "Don't do it!" she said. "Put it back!"

Since we had trained her not to steal, when she came home, she told us about it. She wanted to know why the children had done what they did.

"They think they are getting away with it," I said, "and they will probably get away with it for a long time. Nobody will catch them, and then, all of a sudden, the trouble will come all at once. Then they will wonder why God has forsaken them."

God gets the blame when times get tough.

4. The Thorn Birds

The Thorn Birds is set in the Australian out-back. The story begins in 1915 and centers around Father Ralph, who, after criticizing the bishop, was exiled to the outback to gain common sense and obedience to the church. The plot follows his life and the generations of the people he met there.

One of the climaxes in the TV version of the novel is when the Cleary family, now all adults, is faced with a fire that rages out of control and passes through their sheep ranch. Everything is in turmoil. One of the sons goes out to look for his father and finds that the fire has killed him in the brush. He signals the other searchers by firing his rifle three times into the air. About this time, a wild boar comes out from the underbrush, runs at him, and ends his life. He didn't have time to reload his weapon.

The young man's sister Meggie then comes along and finds him. She reflects on how, in a very short time, she had lost her father and her favorite brother, and how most of her home had been destroyed, except for the house itself.

Father Ralph appears on the scene and tries to console her, but Meggie pulls away. "Why has God done all of this to me?" she asked.

Father Ralph hesitated, searching for something positive to say about the event. Finally, he said, "But Meggie, God brought the rain."

Meggie turned angrily toward the priest. "And who brought the fire?" she demanded.

Father Ralph turned away because he didn't have an answer. He didn't understand the Law of Karma. He didn't understand the wheel of life. He didn't understand that whatsoever we sow, we reap. If he had understood, he would have been able to approach Meggie's question from another viewpoint. If Meggie had understood this principle of spiritual law, she would never have had to ask the question.

5. The Bald Rooster

A letter from Africa told this story:

A hen laid some eggs which had been fertilized by a peculiar rooster. The rooster's head and neck were bald. The bird was such an oddity that the family found it amusing. Every time the rooster came into the yard, they would all laugh at it.

Finally, one day, the eggs hatched. One of the little chicks looked exactly like the rooster. The little thing had a bald head and a bald neck, and because the little chick was so ugly and small, the other chicks picked on him. They picked on him so much that they even broke his leg.

The family saw this and hurried to the rescue. They took the chick into the house and fixed its leg, then decided that the ugly little chick would live inside with the family. The people of that household came to realize an interesting thing. They had laughed at a bald-headed, bald-necked rooster, and now they found that one just like it took up residence in their home.

This story illustrates the laws of karma. In simpler terms, if you have attitudes of any nature, they are going to come home to roost.

6. Throwing Karma

At an ECK picnic, there were two of us throwing the softball on one side and a young fellow by the name of John on the other. John had a good arm, whereas Bruce and I were older. We only had to throw the ball one time to every two of his. Gradually, we began to notice something.

Whenever Bruce threw John a bad ball, John would throw me a bad one back. We found it worked curiously like karma that was one step removed. For instance, when John threw a bad ball to Bruce, Bruce threw him back a good one. John was thinking, Boy, I got off easy. He didn't throw a bad one back. But then when John threw the ball to me, I threw him a bad one back.

That's how we do it. Karma is often round-about like that. If it was always instantaneous, right after the action, people would catch on and break the cycle. It is the delayed reaction that actually makes many believe karma doesn't exist.

7. Soap Opera at Home

There was a time in my spiritual unfoldment, before I became the Living ECK Master, when I would come home from work and share the news of the day with my spouse. As so often happens, we would talk about the private affairs of someone we knew, perhaps a family member who was having a rough time in their marriage. We would speculate on the answers to their problems and go on and on, just like the soap operas.

Two or three days later, my spouse and I would be at each other. I would nag and she would bicker. We came to the conclusion that this was just one of those acts of natural law that was unavoidable. We decided it was natural for a couple to have a little tiff in the house.

After many repeat performances, a realization came to us. We observed that whenever we spoke about someone who was having problems in their marriage, there was a delayed action of about three days, and then it would strike us. The Law of Karma works very strictly to repay the gossipers. Because it took two or three days to come back to us, it took us a while to catch on to the cause of our difficulties.

8. Car Trouble Boomerang

One night I was riding in a car with an ECK friend going to a meeting. My friend told me how he had had his car in the garage earlier that day to make absolutely sure it was in good running order for the trip. He didn't want anything to go wrong because he would be driving me.

As we rolled down the freeway, the man suddenly started to complain about the behavior of one of the persons who would be at the meeting we were to attend, criticizing the individual. I didn't say anything. I just let it be, but then I saw that the temperature gauge on the dashboard was reading hot. "Your engine's overheating," I said.

"What!" he yelled in alarm, seeing that what I had said was true. He quickly pulled onto the shoulder of the roadway. When he raised the hood of the car, he found that the radiator hose had popped off and the water had run out.

Fortunately, I had brought some bottled water with me, and after he reconnected the hose, we poured the water into the radiator to cool it. I knew what had happened.

The driver finally realized the imbalance he created. By letting anger get the better of him, he had caused the condition with his car. These things happen so often. Often there is a lag period of two to three days, or two to three weeks, from the time we have set a negative thought in motion before it comes back to us. Then the effect seems so far removed from the original gossip that we forget what the cause of it was.

9. ECK-Vidya Reading

When Paul Twitchell was the Living ECK Master, he gave an ECK-Vidya reading to an individual who was having problems with frustration and anger. Paul studied this individual Soul's entrance into the lower worlds on the physical plane. He saw that the man first incarnated on another planet, a warlike planet, and then came to earth in another incarnation where he took up a body on the continent of Atlantis. That was about 50,000 years ago. Black magic was very strong there.

The man was the court healer in Atlantis. He was favored by the queen, who recognized his ability to work with the greater power, not the pure spiritual power, but the positive power. The black magicians were angered by this and swayed the king into believing that they had more power than the court healer. Consequently, the healer was betrayed and later murdered by the black magicians. His betrayal had been unknown to the court healer. As a result, he died perplexed. He didn't understand why he had been killed; why he was the victim.

Other lifetimes followed—one in ancient Greece, and the individual ran into a couple of similar situations there. Paul showed the man these situations and others as a series of lives, each one as it had built upon the other, compounding his problem, resulting in the karmic tie which he was faced with today.

19

Each Soul has had many thousands of different lives. The ECK-Vidya reader selects those which pertain to the life today, highlighting those strong traits and characteristics which show the fears and other feelings that make this life easier or more difficult. Paul went through and outlined the entire thing for the man, and at the end he concluded: "Well, since you've come on the path of ECK, you have made great strides in breaking this karma. By the time you finish out this life much of this will be behind you."

10. The Angry Camper

A man was going camping, and he wanted his wife to go with him. She tried to make him understand that camping to her was staying in a motel with a color television and a pool, not roughing it in a tent. He got angry at her and said that he was going anyway and that he was taking his son with him. Then he stormed out of the house and jumped into the car with his young son.

They drove two miles outside the city and found a nice spot in the open country. While he set up camp, his son began to play by himself. Unknown to the father, the boy played with the car keys and unthinkingly threw them into the tall grass and brush.

After they had had their overnight outing and were prepared to return home, the man realized that his keys were missing. The child told him what he had done, and they looked and looked for the keys but couldn't find them. Finally, they walked to a telephone, where he called his wife.

"We're going to be late," he told her. "We have spent the last hour scratching around in the brush looking for the car keys."

She was laughing. She wasn't an ECKist, but she understood the laws of life. She realized that the angry way her husband had stormed out of the house had come back to him. Now he had to very patiently look for the keys.

In reality, it was the key to self-mastery for which he was searching: self-discipline. He was searching for the type of control where, whatever comes up, he wouldn't fly into blind rages. Soul is then in control of emotions, mind, and body. So, when he called with the news that he was searching for the car keys, his wife started laughing. A good wife will laugh. "You know, you had it coming," she said. "That's what you get. That's your payment." She didn't call it karma, because she didn't know it by that name, but she knew the law of cause and effect.

11. Good Housekeeping

Children have their problems too, little things like rooms which seem to get dirty by themselves. My daughter will clean her room, and I am amazed. Sometimes she is not even in the room, and I can see the mess accumulate. Where does it come from?

Blouses will appear on the floor, and every time she cleans up she assures me: "Dad, I'm gonna keep it clean. I'm really going to keep it clean this time."

I am trying to get a lesson across to her, and like every other parent, I feel I am failing. "Do one thing at a time," I explained to her. "If you put something down, clean it up. This is how you go through life, you know. If you are on top of it, you keep things simple. You live moment to moment. You do one thing at a time. This way you can do an amazing amount of work because you never get yourself confused. You set one goal, and then you set another goal, and then another, but they are little, achievable goals."

And then a half-day later, I walked back into my daughter's room. I was amazed how the place had self-destructed. This happened not once, but time after time. I got tired of hearing myself say the same thing, so I didn't say it anymore. Instead I watched. After a day or two the chair in her room was stacked a foot high with clothes. The closet is only two steps to the left, and it is full of hangers, but who bothers with hangers? And the laundry basket, which is where the clothes belong after they have been worn, stands there empty. Sometimes clothes hang over the edge of it.

But that is life. I don't know the answer. I recognize that there are different expectations at work here. One set of expectations is from the parent which says, "Be clean!" The other one from the child which says, "Be alive!" The two have different standards and they don't mix. As a result, Mom finally raises cain. "You don't eat until you clean up your room," she says.

The child believes itself to be the victim of an irate parent and feels that the punishment is unjust. She refuses to clean the room. Parent and child argue. This is how karma is caused.

12. Past-Life Regressions

A psychiatrist, teaching a course in psychology at a local college, was asked her opinion about using hypnosis for past-life regression. The instructor thought a moment, considering the question, and then cited a story of a person who had supposedly been taken back to another time through hypnotic regression.

The regression unfolded a past life which took place during the Second World War. The woman had lived in a German concentration camp and had experienced all sorts of horrible things. The regression turned out to be a severe shock to the woman, the instructor pointed out. "I strongly recommend against anyone looking at his past lives through a method such as hypnotic regression," she said, "because we have enough problems to handle right here and now without borrowing from the past."

Too often we want to live in the imagined splendor of days gone by. We want to know the past because we feel that we were a noble king or queen. We like to believe that we had servants waiting on us hand and foot, and carrying us about on litters. We can picture ourselves being attended to by servants with great fans, fanning us and swishing away the flies. We say, "That is the kind of life which fits me. I know I am something special."

People often want to know about their past lives because they are a failure in the present life.

They are not able to face the problems they have made for themselves here. They have absolutely no idea how to start the creative imagination working inside them. The way to be creative is to practice the Spiritual Exercises of ECK.

13. Cow Paths of the Mind

Three hundred years ago, there was a little calf on its way home. It meandered through the forest, making a trail as it went. The next day, along came a dog. The dog smelled the cow's tracks and followed them. A few days later, along came a bellwether. The male sheep led the flock along the trail made by the calf and the dog. Now there were more tracks through the forest that led to some home.

After a couple of years, men started to track along this path. They bitterly cursed the crookedness of it, but they followed it anyway. Time went on, years passed, and eventually this animal trail became a country road. After more years, it became a city thoroughfare; and finally, after more years, it became the main street of a metropolis. It was still crooked. You had to travel three miles to advance one mile. All the same, the people drove down this crooked street by the thousands, by the hundreds of thousands, day after day. They cursed it and yet they followed this path that was originally made centuries ago by the calf.

In ECK, we understand that the mind forms grooves and runs in a rut. We have habits that we pick up as children. These habits carry into the teen years and gradually harden and solidify as we grow older. These habits form attitudes which often express themselves in anger, vanity, lust, greed, and attachment.

The only thing that is greater than mind is Soul. It alone has the power to nudge mind out of the rut. The path of ECKANKAR makes us aware of Soul. It is not the only path to God, but it is the most direct one.

14. Traveling the Time Track

Imagine yourself on the caboose of a train. There are no other cars behind you, just a station set in the landscape and people. You feel a part of the scene until suddenly the train starts to move. When the train pulls out of the station, you can still see things close at hand, very clearly. As you move away from the station, the landscape and people you first saw when the train was stationary now recede into the distance, becoming smaller and smaller as you move away from them. Because the train you are on is moving, all of what you saw recedes into the distance. Everything becomes fainter and fainter until you can barely see anything. Finally, it all disappears.

Your ride on the train is the present moment. What you are seeing from the caboose is the past. As you move further and further away from it, the shapes recede, becoming smaller and smaller, until finally, you can't see them anymore. What is happening is that as the train picks up speed, it increases the distance between you in the present moment and that fixed event that is in the past. As the train continues into the distance, you can describe less and less and less of the past. Our records of Atlantis and Lemuria are almost non-existent, because they are so far in the past that we can't see them clearly.

We can't see what is going to happen tomorrow to America or Europe, politically and geologically, because to see the future we would have to be at the front of the train, and we are at the back. The future comes up on us unseen. It is for this reason that we must concern ourselves with *now*; to live in the moment. Be aware that you are alive; that you are gaining experience.

15. Whistler's Mother

Around the turn of the century, a painting titled *Arrangement in Grey and Black No. 1: The Artist's Mother* was presented by the artist to the Royal Academy in Britain. The art curators mocked it, shrugging their shoulders in distaste, saying that something aggravated them about the painter's style, and they mocked the title as well.

It was a very simple picture. In the painting, there was a woman in profile seated sideways. She was a quiet looking person with something on her head, and there was very little color to her or to her clothes. The painting was shown only after a member of the Academy threatened to resign if the painting were not exhibited.

Interestingly enough, years later, this painting became recognized as one of the most popular works of art of all time. The masterpiece is now known as *Whistler's Mother.*

The point is this. When a spiritual teaching comes out, such as ECKANKAR, the Ancient Science of Soul Travel, there is a real shock wave in society. A change occurs in the mass consciousness. Today, television series are showing people leaving the body. Movies are showing people leaving the body. People are getting very used to this. The words *Soul Travel* are still considered a bit on the unorthodox side, but in twenty years the Ancient Science of Soul Travel is going to be more commonplace. At that point in the future, people will wonder why there was ever a re-action to ECKANKAR and the Ancient Science of Soul Travel in 1965, '75, and '85.

It is a curious thing. The karmic patterns are speeding up for the human race. As the karmic patterns speed up, the world is under the nuclear threat, geologic changes are occurring, and the economy is on the brink of either making it or not. While all these catastrophes loom on the horizon, people are learning lessons with each other, and the consciousness is rapidly rising. As it rises, people are more willing to be open to ideas which are different from their own. This is the world into which the ECKist comes. This is the world into which you go as the ECK chela, speaking and demonstrating the principles of ECK.

Contemplations...

What is the purpose of Soul? It is to have the experience on this earth of going through everything, through every experience, until one day, Soul becomes a Co-worker with God. Our talents are used in a way we enjoy.

* * *

This is a shocking statement, but we must learn to be totally responsible for all our actions and our deeds and our thoughts.

* * *

The spiritual principle is that you get the most effect out of everything you do and then everything is turned to a spiritual effect. Everything in our life, all the forces, instead of being scattered all over and being wasteful, are aligned through the spiritual exercises in one direction. The direction is toward God, the SUGMAD.

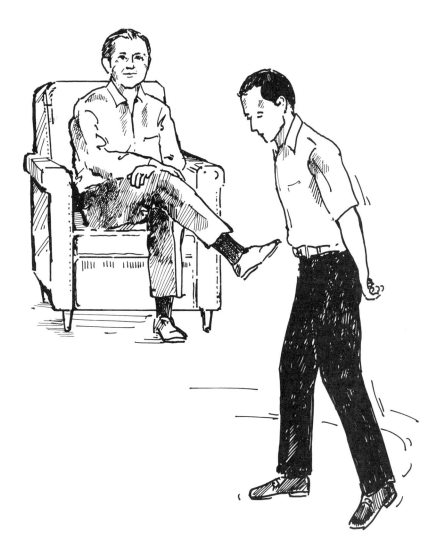

"Paul, when am I ever going to have experiences on the inner planes—with you or with the Sound and Light of ECK?"

Chapter Two

Dreams

16. Audience with Paul Twitchell

During my first year in ECKANKAR, I had a couple of experiences with the Light and Sound of Spirit, the ECK; but the memory quickly faded, and I forgot about it. I began to worry, because it didn't seem that I was having any experiences.

One night as I was drifting off to sleep, I asked Sri Paul Twitchell, who was the Living ECK Master of the time, to help me. As I inwardly expressed this desire, I saw him sitting in an easy chair, watching me. I was pacing the floor in front of him, walking back and forth with my hands behind my back in the classic thinker position. And I said, "Paul, when am I ever going to have experiences on the inner planes—with you or with the Sound and Light of ECK?"

Of course, I didn't realize that it was happening. This was in the dream state, and I believed that I was wide awake. He looked at me for a long while, and then he turned his head to look at a picture of a lady. She had been on the Earth Plane about 199 years, and the picture showed scenes of her entire life. It showed scenes of her childhood, her adulthood, and her many experiences. Paul turned to me again and pointed to the picture. "I don't know how to break this to you," he said. "You are a young man, but even when you get to be this woman's age, it doesn't look good."

I knew it was all over. "Yeah," I said, "the spiritual path is too hard. It doesn't look as if I'm ever going to make any progress on this path to God at all."

Paul just sat there with his arms folded, looking at me. Finally, I walked away very much upset.

Immediately, I woke up in my bed. I was really upset and out loud I asked the question, "When am I going to have an inner experience with the Sound and Light?"

The dream had come about so naturally that it took me nearly half a day to figure it out. The ECK Masters work in subtle ways.

17. Harold and the Purple Crayon

There was a little book which came out a number of years ago, titled *Harold's Purple Crayon*. Someone thought it was fitting and sent it to me. I decided to read it to the children at a seminar. I sat down on the floor with them in the children's room and began.

It was the story of a boy who went into the dream state and actually created his own dream. In his dream he had a purple crayon, and wanting to take a walk, he used it to draw a road so that he would have something to walk upon.

But it was such a long road and not very interesting, so he decided to take a shortcut. He thought about it and then chose a shortcut through a forest. He drew a single tree. He didn't want to make the forest too big, because he didn't want to get lost.

It was a wonderful story. The little person went through it creating his dreams. It showed how Soul goes along and creates whatever It needs to finally get back home.

The little boy always kept his eye on the moon. "Well," he said, "I know the moon is always right outside my bedroom window." So he took his crayon and drew the moon up in the sky, and he kept it there throughout his whole adventure. I explained to the children who were listening that the moon was like the Blue Star of ECK, that it was always with them. Then the boy in the story drew the window around the moon, and he felt very secure. Here I am in my room, because the moon is always right there in the window, he assured himself.

Every once in a while, while I was reading the story, I would pause and hold the book up for the children to see the pictures the boy had drawn with his purple crayon. They would all scramble over to me to get a closer look, all except one child. One little girl sat in the back, and she didn't move. Instead, she called out, "I can't see!"

I wondered why she didn't act like the others and come up closer to see. But I would lean over and hold up the book to her. She'd take a good look at it and finally nod that she was satisfied. Then I'd read another page and hold it up to the other children. Again, she would call out, "I can't see!"

The child was actually acting very much like a grown-up. The nature of children is to enjoy an open communion with the other worlds, but eventually education closes in on us and we lose this openness.

18. The Yellow Tow Truck

A lady ECKist was driving in a rainstorm to meet a friend. It was raining so hard that she drove with her headlights on, even though it was the middle of the day. She drove along until finally she arrived at her friend's apartment and pulled into the driveway. The first thing she noticed was a yellow tow truck sitting out front and that its driver kept looking around very strangely. He glanced at her and then looked up the street and then back at her again.

The lady had a peculiar feeling about his presence although she didn't know why, but she brushed the feeling away, reminding herself of the many apartments in the area. Doubtless he was there to help someone in trouble. She parked the car and got out, once more turning to check on the tow truck. She didn't know why she was struck so strongly by its presence, but she was. He was still there.

She went into her friend's apartment and stayed there, visiting for a couple of hours. They enjoyed a nice, long visit. Several hours later, she returned to her car to find she had left the lights on, and now the battery was dead. She had to arrange to get help from someone with jumper cables, then run the vehicle awhile until the battery gradually recharged itself. She was all right, but it cost her a good deal of trouble.

She wondered about the incident, but it wasn't until the next morning that it finally occurred to her: the ECK had been trying to tell her to turn off her car lights. The ECK had brought a yellow tow truck and parked it right where she couldn't help but see it. What more did she need?

The experience was a waking dream, which is another form of the Golden-Tongued Wisdom. This is a form of the ECK-Vidya working in your daily life. It is having the degree of consciousness expanding outwardly in concentric circles around you, reaching further and further to encompass the knowledge that you need to make better decisions—the knowledge to run your life better.

19. Ladybug, Ladybug

A woman and her daughter were outside enjoying nature when a ladybug landed on the little girl. The child was delighted and immediately recited the poem her mother had taught her. "Ladybug, ladybug fly away home. Your house is on fire" and so on. They laughed about it and stayed out in the sun. Soon a whole bunch of ladybugs came, and the little girl was suddenly covered with ladybugs.

Naturally, the mother and child thought this was pretty cute, and they stayed out in the sun some more. Again and again, they recited the poem "Ladybug, ladybug fly away home. Your house is on fire."

Finally, when they returned home, they found the little girl had a terrible sunburn. The ladybug had been sent by the ECK to show that the little girl's body, her house, was burning. But they had been so caught up in the ladybug rhyme that it never occurred to them that the Golden-Tongued Wisdom of ECK was speaking to them through this form of a waking dream.

This is why I encourage you to always keep your eyes open. Look around you. Once you are linked up with Divine Spirit through the initiations of ECK, Spirit begins to work, to uplift, to strengthen, and to straighten out your life. The only reason you don't realize it more often is that you are walking around with your ears and eyes shut, crying about the injustices that have come to you in life.

When things happen to us, we would rather believe it is someone else's fault, not ours. In ECK, we learn very soon that everything that happens to us is something to teach us more about the laws of Spirit.

Contemplations...

Soul can create whatever It needs.

*   *   *

Our consciousness is expanding outwardly in concentric circles, reaching further and further to encompass the knowledge needed to make better decisions—the knowledge to run your life better.

*   *   *

Once you are linked up with Divine Spirit through the initiations of ECK, Spirit begins to work, to uplift, to strengthen, and to straighten out your life.

*   *   *

In ECK, we learn that everything that happens to us is something to teach us more about the laws of Spirit.

*   *   *

The ECK Masters work in subtle ways.

Fubbi Quantz and I turned and walked further into the God world of two golden suns...

Chapter Three

Soul Travel

20. The World of Two Golden Suns

I was walking with one of the ECK Masters. We were going into a world of golden light. It was a far world which had a beauty beyond description, except to say that everything there was seen through a golden veil.

There were two golden planets in the sky, and since there was no time and no space, they were moving very quickly but they weren't going anywhere. As the planets spun very fast overhead, the ECK Master Fubbi Quantz and I turned and walked further into the God World of two golden suns, but we didn't walk at all.

There was a yearning to go further and further, further than I had ever gone before, because the love of God, the SUGMAD, was drawing me. At one point, Fubbi Quantz turned and said, "You have to go back now, my son." His words were spoken with a great deal of compassion and love. He spoke with the understanding of one who had experienced what I was experiencing. I knew that at one time he, like me, had wished to go on forever and that someone had said to him, "You must go back now, my son."

And so it is when you, too, have to return from the world of golden light. Whether you want to or not, you have to take the expanded consciousness which you have attained into the world of matter. The golden consciousness glows very strongly at first, then gradually it fades. Very often, there is an awful emptiness inside which says, I wish to go further into the heart of God.

It is our sense of responsibility which brings us back. The only way we can ever go further into the heart of God is to face our responsibilities to serve God. This is the paradox that both allows us to grow and gives us the yearning to want to grow.

21. Parachute Adventure

A woman, whose hobby it was to parachute from an airplane, told me the story of her first jump; how it was almost her last.

As she was preparing to leave the aircraft, her instructor checked the parachute that was strapped to her. "Don't forget to arch your back," he reminded. Then he gave her a pat, and she jumped from the plane.

Almost immediately, she pulled the rip cord, as she had been instructed to do. Nothing happened. The parachute didn't open. She pulled again but there was still nothing. What was wrong? "Oh my God!" she screamed, "Please help me!"

While falling, all of a sudden Soul separated from her body; and she found herself above it, above the falling physical body. With the perception of Soul, which is infinite and instantaneous, she could see what the problem was. She had arched her back, as her instructor had told her, but she had arched it too much. The curvature formed a vacuum so that the air pressure was running over the front of her. She didn't have the presence of mind to pull the reserve chute, but she saw what was wrong and straightened her back. With the vacuum gone, the chute came out and opened.

When she got to the ground, she was shaking, remembering the adventure and glad that she had been given a second chance. Before Soul separated from her body, she didn't know what had gone wrong.

It was the first time the woman had an out-of-body experience. As an ECKist, she would learn to have this experience of being in the greater awareness naturally; to live and work in the Soul body so that she could develop mastery of her own life. When we are working from Soul consciousness, we can shape our own destiny.

22. A Visit from Rebazar Tarzs

A married couple from Canada, who were new to the path of ECKANKAR, decided that they would consciously open their home to the presence of the ECK Masters. It was a point they had discussed with each other, agreed upon, and then forgot. What they had done was give permission to Divine Spirit and Its agents to come into their consciousness.

One night, after getting ready for bed, the husband walked across the bedroom to sit down on the cedar chest where he liked to do his contemplation. He sat there for some time, but nothing happened. Although disappointed in the exercise, he felt a strong love for the ECK Masters. As he went to bed, he lay there for a while thinking about and feeling the presence of the Living ECK Master Wah Z, Rebazar Tarzs, and others. He felt very happy and joyful.

As he quickly slipped into the dream state, Rebazar Tarzs, the Tibetan ECK Master, was there, looking at him and laughing. The young man looked at Rebazar and was struck by the sight of his immensely thick, full, rich, black beard. This ECK Master stood about six feet tall and appeared very youthful, although he is known to be quite old. The man knew right away what Rebazar saw that brought the laughter.

Rebazar was looking at a young man trying to grow a beard for the first time. It was all of six weeks old, and it was scraggly with gray spots.

Rebazar laughed and commented in a friendly way at how scraggly the man's beard was, pointing to the gray spots and laughing even harder. And then they talked about some other matters, some serious aspects of the young man's spiritual awakening, after which the man slipped back into regular sleep.

Morning came, and the young man had forgotten about his visit with Rebazar Tarzs until his wife asked, "Did you see anyone in our room last night?"

"No. Why?" he asked.

"Because somebody was sitting on the dresser, a man with a beard," she said.

And then he remembered. She had described Rebazar Tarzs, who had come to show them that once they had opened themselves to Spirit, the messenger would arrive to bring the blessings of God, the SUGMAD. This is the law, the Spiritual Law.

If experiences don't happen for you at first, try again. You may have to work at it. Sometimes you will meet an ECK Master in disguise on the street. You will know this by a feeling of lightness and happiness you have, either when you are with him or when he has left. The happiness is a blessing brought to you in the form of some truth.

23. Doorway to Higher Consciousness

When I was a cameraman in the printing department, I was often called to meetings with other members of the staff. Working with those people was sometimes unbelievably difficult. There were personality quirks and power plays between the pressman and the preparatory department. So I would approach the meeting room and have no idea of what was going to happen on the other side.

Then one day I was shown on the inner planes that every time I walked through a doorway, I was passing through a doorway to heaven. And that was every doorway, as long as I recognized this in my state of consciousness. I decided to experiment with this concept in my daily life.

The next time I approached the meeting room door at work, I declared to myself that I would leave all of my preconceived notions behind; that I would simply walk through the door and enter into a higher consciousness. I was looking for the God Consciousness, although at that time I didn't know what it was.

When I stepped into the room, I paused thoughtfully. I had just declared that I was in a higher state of consciousness. How was I going to treat those at the meeting? From the point of spiritual awareness, I knew that the answer for every question they could fire at me would be at hand. I was learning to be in the childlike state, open to let Spirit bring whatever experience was important. I was tolerant and patient, and I asked, "What do you suggest?"

This technique makes you very aware. It sets up a consciousness similar to that of going on vacation, where everything you see is out of the ordinary and new. When you return home from vacation, back through the door again, your state of consciousness is even higher.

When you assume a goal, acting as if you have achieved it, you next go about figuring out what you can do to achieve that goal. Life then becomes a living, walking, moving set of spiritual exercises, or contemplations.

You can create spiritual exercises as you go about your work. When you declare yourself a vehicle for Spirit, the ECK, that sets all the little atoms going in the right direction. Harmony is the result. Every answer is already at hand, and all that separates you from it is the degree that you can open yourself to ECK.

24. Imaginative Technique

A gentleman told me how as a boy he loved to go to church. In church, he sat with the other people and marveled at the statues of saints standing grandly on high pedestals, some quite near the ceiling. And he thought to himself, How wonderful it would be to stand beside them. So, while the people around him prayed, in the Soul body, he went and stood next to the statues of the saints which stood high, near the ceiling of the church. One day, he told his mother that he loved to go to church, that it was a wonderful experience because he could go up near the ceiling by the statues.

"You mean in front of the altar?" his mother asked.

"No," he said. "I mean up there by the ceiling."

"Don't speak such foolishness," she said.

The boy was still and said no more, but he wondered about his mother's reaction to what he had told her. He had been able to see and feel himself in another place in his imagination. Where imagination goes, there is Soul. He was quite surprised to find that other people who went to church did not go up near the ceiling. And he wondered, what was the point in going to church?

I tell this story to show you how with imagination you too can move into the worlds that lie beyond the physical world. But first, all fear and

guilt must be removed, because guilt and fear
stand between us and our true spiritual heritage.

25. A Gift of Vision

When my daughter was about four years old, I was sitting with her on the floor. All of a sudden, out of the corner of my eye, I saw this little man about six inches tall dressed in green clothes. He went "Shooo...," motioning us to go away.

I looked at my daughter. "Did you just see something?" I asked.

"Yep," she said.

"Well, what did you see?" I prodded.

She told me what she saw.

"Yep, same thing I saw," I said. Then I asked her if she saw things like that very often, and she said she did.

This type of vision leaves us as we grow older, usually by the time we begin elementary school, when everything begins closing in on us. By the time children are eight or nine, they don't see much from the other planes anymore. It becomes even less by the time they reach thirteen or fourteen. Eventually, for most people, this type of sight disappears, unless they learn to keep the eye of Soul open.

26. An ECK Master without a Name

Sometime while traveling on the inner planes, you may meet an old man. The fellow is generally standing outside a farm gate, and he looks like an old codger. He doesn't have a name. He just sits and grumbles and mumbles in what seems an unpleasant way.

When you see him, you will want to turn away. To yourself you say, Good grief! All I need is a black cloud today. I'm on a Soul journey, and I don't want to be bothered with mumbling and grumbling. But this individual is an engaging sort of person, and he will catch you up in conversation. All of a sudden, you'll see that his skin isn't wrinkled, but rather baby pink and smooth as a youth's. He tells you that he has served his time as the Living ECK Master, and that he did it for ninety-one years.

"Oh yeah?" you say.

He smiles and nods. "When the time is right," he said, "I will give you the secrets of health, step-by-step over the weeks, as they are important to you. This will aid your health and will increase your longevity. You will be given these directions, sometimes in a conscious way, sometimes in an unconscious way; but, nevertheless, this secret doctrine will be given to you because you have earned it." Then the old man opens up the gate, goes through it, and walks off with the gait of a young man.

Watching him, you realize that the whole

thing was an act just to let you, the Soul Traveler, decide for yourself. Was this man a part of truth or not? You reflect back, remembering that you would have preferred not to talk to him, but you did. Because you were willing to give up your concepts of what this man might or might not be, then it became clear. The truth came to you in a simple, clear way. It always works like this. Truth is simple.

When the time is right, you will be approached on the inner planes by the ECK Masters with precise instructions and directions that are needed for you to take the next step in your life.

27. How to Go to Bat

When my daughter went out for the softball team, it was midseason. As any player knows, that is a bad time to come on a team, because everybody else is the team and you are not part of it. But at least she was able to catch the ball, and she could hit it okay.

My feeling was to get her ready for next year when she goes into another level of play, where the pitchers pitch faster. I remember it took me a long time to hit fast pitching. In high school and then college, the guys were fast pitchers, very fast, and the higher one goes, the pitching gets faster and better, harder to hit. It was amazing to me the things pitchers could do. They had the risers that started out at the knees. I'd look at the ball, and it would cross over by my chin, only I was swinging somewhere overhead because I never saw it. I found out that I was swinging too late, the way many batters do. Many times too, I didn't turn my wrist right and I'd hit a weak grounder. What I wanted was a good, clean, solid hit so I could get a good batting average.

Finally, I figured it out. When the pitcher was really fast, I had to be nervy enough to stand in there. If the pitcher saw me standing in too tight, he put one in under my chin to frighten me. I had to have courage and stand in there. A real fast pitcher would go into a windmill windup, and as soon as he would start coming around, I learned to bring my bat around too, so that all I had to do was to meet the ball if it happened to be anywhere in the strike zone. Once I felt it there, all I had to do was push, meet the ball and push. Suddenly, I realized I had the pitcher's rhythm, and now I was always ahead of him.

Then I learned to watch the pitchers who threw change cuts. My batting average soared well above 400. I was batting well because I knew how to do it. It got to be fun when I had it figured out.

I was trying to pass all this along to my daughter. I started by pitching underhand to her, straight underhand, and that was good for that year. Then I started pitching the windmill to her very slowly, although to her it was fast. I kept throwing it and throwing it. She wasn't hitting anything because it was too fast, but I didn't say anything.

"Dad, I can't hit it," she said finally.

"Don't worry, keep swinging," I said. "If you don't mind swinging, I don't mind throwing."

Every so often I'd unintentionally uncork a wild one, which hit her. When she'd back away, I'd talk her into standing firm. "You gotta stand in there," I told her. "If the pitcher ever finds out you're chicken, you aren't going to see a ball coming through there again in your whole life. You're never gonna be a hitter, and you won't be on the team." Then I showed her how to get hit accidentally on purpose without getting hurt, because it's a free base and that counts too. I get mileage out of everything, even out of a bad pitch.

I showed her how to spin away and duck at the plate so that the ball wouldn't hit her in the head. "Don't let it hit you in the head," I said.

"Get out of the way."

One day she got up to bat and, finally, she got ahead of me. She brought the bat around and hit this nice deep fly into center. I pitched her another one and she hit another line drive. She was so happy. She had learned how to do it.

This is exactly the point I am trying to get across. I wouldn't stick with you and give you all these techniques on Soul Travel if I didn't know you could do it. I know, because I have done it. I was once out there trying to learn how to bat and I batted wrong. But I worked and worked and worked at it, and I finally figured it out.

My daughter spent a month just batting and trusting Dad that it would work. She had the heart to stand in the way of a couple of balls. She got hit. She had to be tough enough to take the inside pitches. At first she didn't know how to do it very well. She saw the ball coming at her, and she'd run away from it. Then she got a little smarter, and she started to step back. One time she messed up. She was just clear of the ball that was coming inside at the knees. She jumped back and cocked her knee right into the ball.

"I was going to miss you by six inches," I said, "and you stuck your knee into the ball."

I showed her how to slide with a bad pitch, telling her that if she knew it was going to be bad, then she might as well get mileage out of it. Learn how to draw a walk without hurting yourself.

And this is what life is. This is what Soul Travel is. You learn the techniques. Keep working at them, and then you will succeed.

Contemplations...

Soul Travel is simply a means of coming out of the body, or the separation of the spiritual consciousness from the human consciousness. It may be done through the Spiritual Exercises of ECK, when you are ready.

*   *   *

What we want to do is to make you aware of yourself as Soul; to develop the ability of Soul to move beyond the physical body while you are here, alive today.

*   *   *

Invent your own spiritual exercises. Create your own, because you are Soul, and in Soul you are free.

*   *   *

The Soul body needs exercise in order to keep strong, and this is done through the Spiritual Exercises of ECK. In order to keep physical muscles strong, we have to exercise. In order to keep this contact with God open, we have to exercise.

*   *   *

When doing the Spiritual Exercises of ECK, spend time contemplating upon something that is sacred and beautiful to you, and you shall hear the Sound of God.

The man looked up and said, "Well, this ought to be worth something." The proprietor looked at the man, then his wife. He didn't want unhappy customers. "Well," he answered, "how about the next time you come in, you get a free pizza?"

Chapter Four

Harmony

28. Pizza Bounty

A man was going off on a long business trip, and his wife took him to the airport. After they checked in at his airline, they found they had some time to spare. They were both hungry, and so they decided to have a pizza.

They hurried to the far end of the terminal to a pizza parlor, went in, and sat down. They waited a few minutes and then the proprietor came over and talked to them. He told them that his oven wasn't working correctly and that it would be at least fifteen minutes before he could make them a pizza. Of course, the couple didn't have that much time to spare, but instead of mumbling and grumbling to the proprietor over their disappointment, the man looked up at him and said, "Well, this ought to be worth something."

The proprietor looked at the man, then his wife, and back to the man again. He didn't want to have unhappy customers. "Well," he answered, "how about the next time you come in, you get a free pizza?"

The couple said that would be fine.

The proprietor wrote his offer on a business card and told the man to bring it in the next time he was at the airport and he would give him a free pizza.

When the man got back from his trip, he took the card, presented it at the pizza parlor and got a free pizza. The proprietor was happy because he could make a customer happy, and the customer left happy. They were both well served. It never hurts to ask, because someone might say, "Yes."

Life might say "Yes" too. Many times the bounties of the Holy Spirit are held back from us because we don't ask. We want something to come into our lives, and we just sit and wait. But if we ask for it, we may just get it.

29. The Ski Rack

A man bought himself a car, but on the way home he realized that he should have had a ski rack put on before he drove it off the car lot. He knew it was too late now. The deal was complete, and he had already paid the price. He had no more bargaining power. Yet, on the way home, he couldn't stop thinking to himself how he wished he had a ski rack.

Later he visited a friend, and as he was leaving, he saw a ski rack in the trash pile. "Wow!" he called out in surprise, "You ask the ECK and here it is!" He asked his friend if he could have the ski rack. His friend said, "Sure," but explained that it was not in very good condition.

When he got the rack home and looked at it closely in the light, he saw that it was not in good condition at all. The rubber molding, which was supposed to fit snugly against the car, needed to be glued down. The suction cups were off, and the whole thing was rusty.

He wondered why the ECK had given him such an unsightly ski rack for his new car. He had a happy relationship with the Holy Spirit and began having an inner conversation with Spirit about it. "You know, it is true," he said to Spirit, "I didn't say how good the ski rack had to be."

In a few days, before he could get the old ski rack cleaned up and put on his car, his father-in-law visited. "By the way," his father-in-law said,

"I've got this ski rack and it's brand new. I wonder if you would like to have it?"

And, of course, the younger man's face lit right up.

30. Giving Another Psychic Space

A two-year-old boy named Jeddie was eating a chocolate bar in the living room with his dog Sam. The boy's grandfather was also there, sitting in his easy chair watching television. Lying next to Grandpa's chair was his dog Rags.

Jeddie was having a grand time with his candy bar, and it was smeared all over his face, running down the sides of his mouth. Naturally, Sam wanted to help and started cleaning Jeddie's face for him with enthusiastic licks. Jeddie didn't mind. He liked Sam (which he pronounced *Tham*), and he knew the dog liked chocolate.

Grandpa, looking up from the television, saw this and quickly rose from his chair. Jeddie paused, watching his grandfather stand up. He was a tall, heavyset giant of a man who frequently joked with Jeddie about his bald head, telling the boy that he had no hair because he had so many brains they pushed his hair right out of his head. Only this time his grandfather wasn't smiling, and Jeddie knew he wasn't going to joke with him. Instead, with a great swoop of his hand, the giant man smacked Jeddie's dog Sam across the room.

Little two-year-old Jeddie jerked his head up, staring hard at his grandpa. "Grandpa!" he called out.

"Yeah, Jeddie?" Grandpa answered.

"Rags your dog?" the boy asked, looking in the direction of the old canine, who was watching them from beside Grandpa's chair.

"Yes, Rags is my dog," Grandpa answered, not knowing where Jeddie was going with his questioning.

"Do you hit Rags?" little Jeddie asked.

"No, I don't hit Rags," Grandpa answered.

"Tham is my dog, " Jeddie said. "Don't hit Tham!" Then the little-bitty guy kicked his grandfather as hard as he could in the shin.

This story illustrates the invasion of a person's psychic space and how little Jeddie settled the question. There are, however, many other ways of intruding in someone's psychic space, and often it is done in conversation.

Someone will make a statement, telling you something that is really precious to him. "You know," he will say, "this and this and this happened and so on. . . . " And immediately you add on top of what he said, "Not only that but also. . . . " This is a form of contradiction, and it is a way of putting a little wall around the other person's thoughts. What you are saying in effect is "Your thoughts are okay, but I have a better one and I am going to build it on top of yours."

Usually, it is not our intention to intrude in another's psychic space and yet we do it. I suggest that you consider one point. When you really love another person, you are more apt to listen to what he or she says and are less apt to interrupt with your own version of what the other person is talking about.

31. Finding Heaven in Hell

When I was in the service and it was my time for KP duty, I'd ask to scrub the pots and pans. Of course, no one objected because it was considered absolutely the dirtiest job and nobody else wanted it. But I learned that scrubbing the pots and pans allowed me to be my own man. The mess sergeant didn't holler at the one scrubbing pans because he knew it was the lowliest job. All I had to do was get the grease off, and he would leave me alone.

It didn't take me long to catch on to the benefits of doing the dirtiest job. Not only did the sergeant leave me alone, but I didn't have to be at work as early as the others.

Once in a while I had the bad fortune to be assigned to the food or dessert line. It was a job which everyone else liked. There was no work to it. You put out the food or desserts, and then you'd stand there waiting for the tray in front of you to empty. When the tray became a little bit low on Jell-O, you'd make another trip back to the cooler, get another tray, and walk back out front with it. Of course, while you were in the kitchen, if no one was around, you would help yourself to a couple of olives. Then you would wipe off your mouth so no one would know and go back out front again.

This is how Soul gains experience, by learning to get along in the world. I learned that there was an easy way and there was a difficult way, and that heaven can be found in someone else's hell. One learns to live in a way that no one else can. The Spiritual Exercises of ECK raise the consciousness so that a person can live in a hut and feel as if he were living in a palace.

Where a person lives in the physical world does not tell where he lives in Spirit. There have been many kings who were so impoverished in Spirit that they couldn't wait until spring so they could mount up with their men to cross the borders of the next kingdom for battle. They attacked their neighbors because they felt they just had to have their land. A leader of this nature is afflicted with spiritual poverty.

32. Practicing the Presence of God

In Paris, in 1666, there was a cloistered monk named Brother Lawrence. He was the monk in charge of washing the pots and pans at the monastery. He liked his job because he found it easy to practice the presence of God while doing such very lowly things as scrubbing pots and pans. The monks around him, however, couldn't really understand why he was getting such a thrill out of doing the dirty work. Brother Lawrence didn't care that they teased him, because he saw God in everything he did.

33. The Other Side of the Rope

One afternoon a travel-magazine writer and his daughter were trying to figure out what they wanted to do. Since he knew she liked baseball, he asked: "How would you like to go see the Texas Rangers play?"

"No, thanks, Dad," the little girl said.

"Why not?" the father asked, surprised.

"Because," the girl answered, "I'd rather be on the other side of the rope."

The man stared at his daughter, studying her, trying to understand what she meant. He knew she loved baseball. What did she mean she would "rather be on the other side of the rope"? Was *rope* the latest slang term? He asked her about it.

"Remember last summer when little sister and I went to see the filming of 'Dallas'?" she asked.

He nodded, waiting for her to continue.

She explained that during the filming, a rope had been put up around the set to keep the spectators back. She had stood behind the rope with the rest of those watching, as the film crew ran back and forth on the set. It was really hot that day, and everyone, including the actors, was sweating under the light reflectors on set. All the same, that day she decided, then and there, that if ever she had a choice, she would rather be doing things than watching them being done. Finally, she summed it up. "I'd rather be playing baseball than going to a baseball game," she said to her dad.

The little girl had recognized that there were two approaches to life — the active and the passive. Although watching was fun, given a choice she knew the real fun was participating in the game of life. Being passive is often procrastination, and it is easy to become attached to this state. It is important to break the attachment, which comes with the procrastination, that holds Soul in the lower worlds. I am trying to give you the inspiration to find out how to live life and to enjoy it.

There will be times when troubles come, but this is how the game works. As Soul, you owe it to yourself to participate in the experience of going into life and getting the richest, fullest experiences that you can.

34. A Spiritual Fallacy

It was considered a privileged life to live within the boundaries of the temples in ancient Egypt. The training was long, the pay was poor, and yet many came and most were allowed to stay.

The priest greeted those who came to the temple gates and welcomed them in. "Why sure," he would say. "You can come on in. You want to be a monk and later a priest? Okay." And the person would go through a training period of five or ten years and in some cases longer, before one day the priest would say, "You go back out into the world now. Just go out there and live life. We'll call you when we need you; when there is an opening."

The monk, of course, was shocked. He had meant to devote his entire life to the temple. Now, suddenly, he was told to leave and begin a career in the world. He staggered out into the street completely bewildered.

After a couple of years, the monk got the hang of living within society. He married and eventually had a family. As time went on, his business went well and he developed many friendships. Because people respected him, he was chosen as a community leader and elected to government office.

Suddenly, word would come: "It is time for you to return to the temple."

In those days when you were called, you literally gave up everything for the Master or God.

When we enter the world, we take on responsibilities. By accepting them, we unfold spiritually. There is no quick way. We are not to give up our responsibilities and escape from life secluded in a monastery. If you have a family, you are responsible to that family. Sometimes a person will have difficulty getting along with his spouse and try convincing himself to the contrary. "It is time to go and join a religious order," he might rationalize. "I can't stand my wife anyway." And then the person leaves, thinking that by giving his life to God the problem is solved. This is shirking responsibility. This is not the way.

35. The Adventurer

There was a man who devoted his whole life to a series of adventures. He wanted to ride an elephant, chase an ostrich, and many other things that wouldn't buttonhole him into the routine and boredom of everyday living. He didn't want to be just another nine-to-five person.

This man set a series of goals for himself, and they entailed visiting one country after another. He took a boat trip down the Amazon. Later, he told how river bandits had seen him paddling along in his boat and began taking shots at him. Finally, when he came out into the Atlantic Ocean, he said that if he had known beforehand the dangers that were going to meet him, he never would have done it.

All the same, the man was living a life filled with joyous adventure. Even if you are living a nine-to-five life, you can make it an adventure too. We owe it to ourselves to live life to its fullest in whatever we do. The motivation to do this must come from within.

36. The ECK Way to Pray

An executive was put in charge of a computer company that was about to fold because it was a poor cost center. After a year on the job, the contracts for the company tripled. I knew the man and was curious. I asked him how he had brought this about.

"Before I do anything," he said, "or make any decision at all, I pray to God."

"All right," I said, "but there are many people who pray to God in the wrong way. They ask for control over other people to achieve their own wishes, like the basketball team that is going out to play ball and they pause to pray together. They say, 'Dear God, please help us win!' On the other side of the court, the other guys are busy praying, 'Dear God, help us win!' Do you mean that kind of prayer?"

"No," the executive answered. "I pray only in this way. I ask that I be aware of what the situation is and what the problems are, and I ask for help in whatever way God sees fit."

This executive actually has the attitude of the ECKist. He looks to see what he can do to make the thing work and how he can overcome the problems at hand. He is learning. Soul is unfolding, gaining experience to mature. This is the way to become a fit Co-worker with God. The executive knew how to pray. His prayers were clear prayers.

There is nothing wrong with prayer. It is merely that prayer done by most people is wrong because it is set up to control others' actions. For most, prayer is either to make others go to church or to make others believe in their savior, etc. That type of prayer is wrong. It is an effort to manipulate the actions of others, and, actually, it is playing with black magic.

37. Snails in the Garden

We have a little, bitty backyard garden. I planted flowers, and then the snails found the flowers. This year I didn't bother with too many vegetables because last year the snails found those too. When I go traveling and then return home, I can see how busy the snails have been. So I take an empty, plastic milk carton and a shovel and search them out from their hiding places underneath a little wooden railing in the wooden fence around the garden. Carefully, I scoop them up with the little shovel and dump them into the milk carton. When the carton is full, I call to my daughter, "Find a good place for these snails."

My daughter quickly answers my call and hurries over to take the carton, peeking inside to see how many snails I have collected. It's easy to see that she likes the snails. She'll take one out and admire it, watching patiently until it slips its head out of its shell. She thinks they are so cute with their antennae on the top of their heads.

The snails eat up my whole garden. My daughter doesn't really care because she thinks they are so cute. That's why I give her the job of finding some place away from my garden for them to live. "I don't want to know where you put them," I told her, "just don't put them in the neighbor's yard."

Then a three-week trip came up. I knew that if I didn't do something about the snails, by the time I got home, the flowers and tomatoes I had just planted would be destroyed. I had an idea. It seemed reasonable that snails wouldn't like pepper.

I went to the grocery store and bought a large amount of pepper. Then I went home and sprinkled it all over the plants in the garden. The next morning, just before I left, I hurried outside to see that everything was all right. I was relieved to find that the pepper hadn't harmed the plants and that, so far, there weren't any snails. I considered that the pepper might not only keep away the snails but also my neighbor's cats who were always digging in the flower beds. With this thought in mind, I gave everything a double-dose and sprinkled even more pepper all over the plants.

When I went back into the house, I started sneezing and couldn't stop. At first, I couldn't figure out why, and then I realized that I had pepper all over my clothes. No plan is perfect.

There is a principle to this story. How do you handle things as humble as snails and cats? The answer is that you do the best you can. You use all your expertise. Sometimes you win and sometimes you lose. Sometimes the snails win. Sometimes the cats win. We do the best we can.

38. Four Square Wheels

On the wall in a college philosophy department is a cartoon of two men, one pulling and the other pushing a cart. The two men are really struggling, and it is easy to see why. The cart that they are pulling and pushing has four square wheels. Oddly enough, the cart is loaded with four more wheels, only these are round. If they would just put the round wheels on the cart and the square ones in it, there would be no problem.

The cartoon is an example of the mental man, the intellectual man, groping around in the spiritual worlds. He has absolutely no understanding of the laws. None. So what does he do? He makes fun of something he can't understand, something which is beyond his sight and hearing.

People who experience the Light and Sound of God are not very often the orthodox church people. Rather, they may be people who live in Malaysia or perhaps Africa, where the ancient religions of animism are taught. These religions are misunderstood by people in the West and brushed off as mere worship of nature spirits. This is not true. Those animistic religions are aware of the Light and Sound of God. These people also see the Blue Light of ECK. They don't call it the Blue Light of ECK, but they know that the Light as well as the Sound comes to them in times of trouble and helps them.

39. The College Student's Surrender

There was a college student who had been on the path of ECK for some time. For some reason or another, the spiritual tests which were thrown at her became so difficult that she decided to step back from the outer activities, but she continued with her spiritual exercises. However, it was a time of the dark night of the Soul. During this time she had no assurance whatsoever that there was any such thing as Divine Spirit.

The young lady had set it in her heart to gain admission to one of the large prestigious universities. She didn't have the money, but she applied for a government loan, and because her grades had been good, she was hopeful.

One day she went to the registrar's office to find out if the loan had gone through. The registrar sadly shook her head. The loan had been denied.

The student was beside herself. She had been an excellent student, and yet her way was blocked. There was nothing more she could do, and so she gave up. She would not get her master's degree in communications. Without the loan, she knew she could not afford it.

The registrar suggested that she wait a few more days to see if something came up, but the student knew that nothing could save her now. She had given up trying. She had given up to life. She had stopped buzzing around blindly.

Just as she totally gave up, there was an opening of the creative centers within her. She opened up as Soul so the ECK power could flow in. A few days later, the registrar called her and told her that instead of a government loan, she had obtained a special grant for her, and the grant did not require repayment as the loan would have.

This incident proved to her that there was power in Spirit. I am not saying that when we do the spiritual exercises and we want more money, we merely throw up our hands and say, well this is it. It doesn't work that way. The path is spiritual unfoldment. This means simply learning ways to make ourselves a clearer vehicle for Spirit. This is all we are trying to do. Once the college student had surrendered to Spirit, then the plans which she had carefully laid out for herself were fulfilled.

Spirit works with each person in a way that is right for that person. For someone who has his attention in the spiritual planes, the answer will come on a spiritual level. If you are interested only in greedy accumulation, don't expect Spirit to fill your hat.

40. A Wood-Carver Who Lost the Creative Flow

In the hilly regions of Australia there was a man living in the national forest who did all kinds of wood carvings. He opened his home to visitors, and so you walked up to the gate, paid your money, then followed the path to his house. It was his workplace. You walked through the front door and there he was, standing quite still, like the carvings in his display. His face was very red. It was almost as if someone had painted his face red. It was the redness of anger.

We went on past him and studied his carvings. They were both inside the house and outside in the garden, around fountains and foliage. Carvings of little people seemed to be running through the foliage.

We learned something about the man. He was now eighty-three. Sometime during the span of his life he lost the spark of Spirit in his work. His personal morality or concepts caused a blockage, and when this happened, suddenly his artwork came out in a lower form.

In his earlier work, the man's carvings captured the life of the aborigines. The carvings of bushmen and the women and the animals were very much alive. His creation had been of living things in motion. But when he lost his contact with Divine Spirit, the man became frantic and turned to religion. He became a modified orthodox Christian, and his life turned angry and bitter. He became extremely bigoted about certain races. His work changed completely.

Instead of depicting life in his carvings, he now depicted death. He carved the images of animals after they had been killed. His attitude toward the aborigines was not the same. He now envisioned himself the savior of these people, and he even carved an image of himself on a cross. In doing so, he had exercised vanity of the most unimaginable kind.

This unfortunate change came about in the man when he put qualifications on what Spirit was trying to express through his artwork. Spirit was trying to lift him higher, beyond his creations of the aborigines, but he couldn't sidestep mind and its opinions and go further. Because he couldn't, he fell back into the base prejudice now seen in his later work.

41. Survival: A Study of Color

There was a lady who worked as a motel maid. Her husband didn't mind her working because she earned extra money, but he traveled and when he was home, he liked her to be home with him. This presented a problem. It wasn't always easy for her to shift her schedule to meet his. To do so often meant that the entire work schedule for the whole housekeeping staff had to be adjusted. It wasn't easy because the other maids had their own lives to think about— vacation times, weekends, etc.

The woman felt she was pushed into a corner. She wanted to keep her marriage, and she also wanted to keep her job, which signified independence to her. Gradually, she became aware that when her supervisor was wearing light pink, bright or light yellow, or some other happy color, she could request a schedule change with positive results. She also learned that if her supervisor was wearing some sort of dark, dreary color—brown with lavender stripes or something similar—that it was not a day to ask. When the supervisor wasn't feeling particularly good about herself, she wore dark colors. When she was happy and easygoing, she wore light ones.

The woman believed her observation to be a mere study in color, but actually she had gained this knowledge through the inner teaching, the secret teaching. The knowledge had come to her so naturally that it hadn't occurred to her that there was anything unusual about it. Actually, it came to her from Spirit to use as a survival tool.

42. The Overcrowded House

Chester Karrass, author of a book called *Give and Take,* told an interesting story about a woman in a Russian village who sought the assistance of a wise man who lived nearby.

"I've got a problem," the woman told the wise man, "a serious problem with my family. We live in a little hut, and there is barely enough room for my husband, myself, and our two children, but hard times have forced my in-laws to move in with us."

The sage thought about the woman's problem for a long time before answering. "Do you have a cow?" he asked finally.

"Yes," the woman answered.

"If the house is very crowded and you are finding this a difficulty," he said, slowly and carefully, "I can show you how this problem can be taken away from you so that you can find happiness."

"That would be wonderful," she said, feeling some relief.

"Take the cow into your house to live with you," the wise man instructed. "And come back to see me in a week."

The woman thought about the sage's instructions. It was a very small house, and to have a cow in it seemed very uncomfortable as well as strange. However, the woman knew that the wise man had a very good reputation, and so she went home and brought the cow into the house.

The cow was a nuisance. Every time the cow turned around, the family had to jump off the chairs, which were already pushed up against the wall, and climb over the cow to get to the chairs on the other side of the room. It was a small hut, and the woman realized that this didn't make any sense at all.

The next week she returned to the sage and told him of the overcrowded conditions in their hut. "The cow is a nuisance. We can't even eat because the cow is there. We can't sleep. Every time it's quiet, the cow will moo."

"Do you have any chickens?" the sage asked.

She was a little hesitant but she said, "Yes, I have some chickens."

"Take the chickens into the house with you," the sage instructed. "And come back and see me in a week."

The woman was about to tell the sage what he could do with the cow and chickens but instead she held back, telling herself that she had only given the sage one chance. She would try again. So she went back home and took the chickens into the house. It was just a mess. Every time the cow turned around, the family jumped for the other chairs, which frightened the chickens and they would fly in the air and the feathers would get into the soup. The in-laws were fighting, the husband was screeching, the cow was turning around, and the chickens were squawking. It was the worst situation the woman had ever experienced.

At the end of that week, the woman was beside herself. She hurried off to see the sage. "I've had it!" she yelled at the wise man. "The in-laws are difficult enough, but with the cow and the chickens, it is just too much!"

The wise man studied the woman. "All right," he said, calmly, "if it would make you happier, take out the chickens."

The woman went back home and took the chickens out of the house. A week later she returned to the sage and said, "You know, I am much happier. It's much better without the chickens in the house. They don't cackle the first thing in the morning, and the children aren't fishing feathers out of their soup."

"Well, I am happy to hear that," the wise man said. "Now you can go home and let the cow out of the house too."

The woman was so pleased and relieved. She returned home and let the cow out of the house. From that moment on, she, her family, and the in-laws lived happily ever after.

You are wondering what kind of a spiritual point there is to the story. You think about it. I am going to let it hang, like waiting for the other shoe to drop. See what you come up with.

Contemplations...

If you want something from life, first of all, you have to earn it, but you also have to be open to the gifts.

* * *

Many times the bounties of the Holy Spirit are held back from us because we don't ask.

* * *

The mere fact that you can identify a problem means that within you, you have the solution to the problem.

* * *

The quest for God is the quest for true happiness.

* * *

We are Soul. This life is an opportunity for Soul to get rich experiences in any way that It can. I am speaking about uplifting, constructive experiences, the kind where we find ways to serve all of life.

* * *

Thoughts are things, and it is important to keep thoughts of a spiritual nature, where we put attention on living a life that is a clear step toward growth.

* * *

As you grow in spirituality, your whole life must improve.

* * *

Sometimes the ECK may work in a gentle way. It may give you just a nudge, a feeling of how to act, what to do, which dentist to go see. Something right down to earth.

* * *

There is room in ECK for the doubter because, as you express and exercise your doubts, you gain in strength. If you are the type of person who has to have something proven to you, you'll have it proven to you.

* * *

In the spiritual consciousness, we know that there is always an answer for every situation that comes up in our life. There is always a way, somehow. What holds us back is our attitudes.

* * *

And finally you run out of words and simply say *Life Is, ECK Is,* or *Spirit Is.* Life is beyond eternity.

Holding both dogs in one arm, she grabbed her flashlight, shining it in the direction of the giant footsteps. She
came suddenly eye to eye with her monster.

Chapter Five

Psychic Traps

43. A Night in the Wilderness

On the airplane from San Francisco to Amsterdam, I met a lady and we got to talking. She told me how she loved to go camping, backpacking way back into the forest where there were no people and where it was very quiet. She loved the quiet and peace and harmony that this contact with nature brought her. And she took her two small dogs with her.

On one particular trip, the lady and her dogs hiked way back into the forest and made camp next to a stream. Then she built a campfire, and both she and the dogs ate and settled down for the night. She stretched out under the stars without even a tent. Everything was quiet and peaceful. As the brook murmured in the stillness, it gave her company. It sounded like people talking in the distance, and she gradually went to sleep very peacefully.

During the middle of the night, she awoke with a start. She heard huge giantlike steps coming through the forest, and they were coming to where she was camped. As they came closer and closer, she grew absolutely terrified. The sounds of rustling leaves were coming upon her.

Quickly she grabbed up her two little dogs. She didn't want them to go out and foolishly attack the monster. Holding both dogs in one arm, she reached over, grabbed her flashlight and turned it on, shining it in the direction of the giant footsteps. She came suddenly eye to eye with her monster. A little field mouse stood staring back at her.

When the lady turned on the flashlight, it was like turning on the light of ECK. The light gave her the bit of information she needed to take away her fear. The insight which ECK gives takes away the ignorance and with it, the fear. Once ignorance and fear are removed from our lives, then we enter into the freedom of Soul. We can then come into the states of wisdom, power, and freedom.

44. The Hang Glider

There was a man who loved to fly. He owned a hang glider, and whenever he got the urge, he'd tow it to a cliff, set it up, and take off, soaring from the mountaintop. Since he was unafraid and comfortable that no misfortune would come to him, it was not unusual for him to set off on his adventures alone. But one day he brought a friend with him. His friend had never flown a glider, and that day there was a strong wind blowing. The man who owned the glider summed up the situation and gave his friend some instruction, but his friend was so excited and anxious that he paid little attention. After he was strapped into the harness, he took off running with his wing tipped high, and as soon as he got to the edge of the cliff, the wind caught the wing and blew him back.

The man who was the experienced hang glider pilot watched his friend, then said, "Remember, when you run into the wind, dip your wing down a little. If you don't the glider could flip back on you."

His friend nodded that he understood, then he straightened himself under the glider and backed up. A moment later he ran toward the cliff, but again he neglected to keep the wing down. A gust of wind caught him, lifted him into the air, and sent him somersaulting back across the field. He and the glider went bouncety, bouncety, bounce off into the distance.

111

The man who owned the hang glider went running after him until finally the glider stopped. But before he reached the glider, his friend, who was stunned by the mishap, unthinkingly unhooked the safety harness. The glider had no weight to hold it, and it blew off with the wind.

The glider owner hesitated. He had a decision. Should he help his friend or go after his hang glider? Very quickly he decided that his friend showed no signs of injury and could wait for attention until he returned. So he ran after his hang glider which he knew could be destroyed. Finally he caught it, secured it to himself, and brought it back to where his friend was waiting.

His friend had been watching the chase and shook his head as he saw him return with the glider. "You know," he said, "that thing is really dangerous. You shouldn't ever come out here by yourself. Look what happened to me. If you had been up here alone, you may have been hurt and there would be no one to help you."

The fellow with the hang glider studied his friend in disbelief. It was not he who didn't know how to hang glide. His friend had failed because he wouldn't pay attention to how it was done, and now he was trying to attach his fears and insecurities onto him. "Understand one thing," the pilot finally said to his friend, "I came here to fly, not to fall."

The man who owned the glider had a different outlook on life than his friend. He focused on the moment. When he was about to jump off the cliff in his glider, he thought only of that, flying. He never thought of what might happen if he didn't do it correctly. He had learned how to operate his glider, and he had confidence that he could operate it safely. So he focused his attention on the safety rules he had come to trust. His friend, on the other hand, did not pay attention to his instructions, and then, when he failed in his attempt to fly, he rationalized that the sport of gliding was unsafe.

If you want to fly, fly! If you have fears that are holding you back, you will get the wing too high in the wind. Fear will cause you to go bouncing back and back, and it will leave you in a tangled wreckage. We are really talking about the experiences of life. In that sense, exercise courage in doing what it is you want to do. Be cautious without being fearful.

45. The Confessional

Sometimes religious leaders put guilt in one's path. In this story, a fourteen-year-old boy went to the priest for confession.

"What have you come here to confess?" the priest asked.

"Nothing," the boy said. "I have no sins."

"That can't be," the priest said. "Think harder."

The boy couldn't think of anything, but the priest was persistent. He had never known anyone to come to him who had never sinned.

"You must tell me something," the priest said.

"Well, I fight with my brothers," the boy said finally. "And sometimes I say bad words."

"What words?" the priest asked.

"Just bad words," the boy answered. He didn't really use bad words. He was merely saying it to please the priest. Then he said, "Forgive me, everything I told you is a lie."

"Well, that is very bad. You must do penance, my son," the priest said.

And the young boy was directed to walk down this big, long church aisle and go to the front of the people and do penance. And he said, "Dear God, forgive me, but the priest made me lie."

46. The Pedicab

A writer of books on the occult and Eastern religions was traveling in India. He had made arrangements for a cab to pick him up and take him to the train station, but something happened and he missed the cab. Quickly he negotiated with the operator of a pedicab (a pedal-driven tricycle). They came to an agreement on price, and the writer climbed in back with his luggage. The cyclist peddled away.

As they went along, the writer began to notice that the cyclist was showing signs of fatigue. He peddled harder and harder, laboring in such a way that it appeared that he may have a heart attack if he continued up the street. The writer suddenly felt very guilty. Here he was with all his luggage in the little cart, working the cyclist to death.

The further they traveled, the worse the cyclist seemed to get, until finally, the writer felt so ashamed that he wanted to jump off the cart and yell for the cyclist to stop. "Hey, you ride and I'll peddle," he nearly called out, but before he did, they arrived at the train station.

The weary cyclist dismounted and the Westerner stepped down from the cart. Nearby, there were Indian men sitting around watching. They exchanged glances and conversation with each other as the cart drove up. It was obvious they wondered how much of a tip their Indian friend, the cyclist, would receive.

As would be expected, the writer, who was from another country, was so guilt-ridden that he overtipped the cyclist. The watching Indian men gave each other knowing glances, winking at each other. It was obvious they admired the bike pedaler, and it was also obvious that they scorned the traveler.

The traveler realized that he had been caught by his feelings. He turned to the cyclist and gave him a hard stare. "Guilt is the meat of this transaction," he said resentfully, then went on his way.

So often guilt is the meat of our transactions. An example of this is a person who overtips in a restaurant after receiving bad service. A tip is expected. If we don't do it, we are working against the social consciousness and we'll go home feeling as though we haven't done our duty. This feeling of guilt has been bred into us, not just in this life but also in past lifetimes. Wherever we walk and whatever we do, we have the clouds of guilt hanging over us. Many of these feelings are unconscious memories from past lives. They come with us and they are chains on Soul. Guilt wastes our resources and causes us to do things against our will. Is it any wonder that there is unhappiness and poverty in the world? Our energies are not directed in a straight line towards our goal but are sidetracked by guilt.

47. The Rope Trick

A counselor on a ranch for the mentally retarded was put in charge of a young boy. The boy was to stay with him at all times. That was okay, because the counselor liked the little guy and found him quite agreeable, except for one thing. The young boy disappeared on him every time he turned his back. When he would turn around the little guy would be gone.

At first he didn't know what to do about it, but then he had a flash of inspiration. He got a rope, tied it around his own waist, and gave the end of the rope to the little boy to hold. The little boy never again ran away, because now the counselor was his prisoner.

When the end of the summer came and camp was out, the counselor went home and thought about the incident and then wrote to me. "You know," he said in his letter, "the negative power has me in the same state. The rope that is tied around the waist of the negative power has five strands—anger, lust, greed, attachment, and vanity. What am I doing, standing here like a fool, holding onto this rope?"

The counselor realized that all he had to do was drop the end of the rope and he was free. As soon as he realized this, he took a giant step in spiritual unfoldment.

48. A Trapped Fly

When you have a daughter in grade school, mealtime is not all brown rice and veggies. After school one day, we stopped at a fast-food restaurant for a hamburger. We sat down at one of the booths, and while we were eating, I noticed a fly buzzing around. It was obvious that the fly felt that it was caught inside the restaurant. It flew back and forth in a frenzied sort of way, and every once in a while, it would speed up and go smack into the plate-glass window. It hit this invisible barrier which was completely beyond its comprehension.

After it bounced off the window, it would fall down onto the sill to recuperate. When it got its strength back, it would take off again and bang into another plate-glass window. It would hit the glass, bounce off, and then start all over again. I was sitting there, shaking my head. "You know," I said to my daughter, "there is just no getting away from spiritual lessons, not even long enough to have a hamburger."

My daughter stared at me oddly for a moment, then at the fly, and shrugged her shoulders like she didn't understand.

"Isn't that just like life?" I began again. "We're just like that fly. We take off. We don't know the first thing about the laws of Spirit, and we go head-on full speed into an invisible barrier. We get banged on the head. We fall down. We cry. Of course, being human, we are beyond the

121

fly. The fly just gets up and takes off and does the same thing all over again. As humans, we are different. We pray. We blame God. Sometimes we don't blame God. We just say, "God, I don't know where this came from but please take it from me."

Someday, if the fly is lucky, it is going to think and wait until a customer walks in the door; if it could understand the grand concept of a door that looks just like a plate-glass window.

I thought of helping the fly, but it was going too fast. We couldn't catch it because there were other people around trying to eat their food, and to chase a fly in a restaurant isn't polite. Anyway, the fly is trying to learn the laws of Spirit just as we are.

49. Astral Entities

A married couple wanted spiritual growth. In their search for spiritual truth, they joined a church group in which the leaders acted as channels for entities from the Astral Plane.

One day an entity spoke through one of the church leaders and claimed to be Jesus. It introduced the leader to a spirit named Emmanuel and said that Emmanuel was to be the spirit guide for the couple who had only recently joined the group. The couple, anxious to learn more, opened themselves to this very low force. They dedicated themselves to strengthening the bond that this entity had with them and allowed it to run their lives.

"What may we do to serve?" the couple asked Emmanuel.

"You have now come to the point in your spiritual life when you can give your home," the entity Emmanuel told them. "Give the house you now live in to the church members. Ten of them will move in and live there."

Fortunately, the couple had two houses. They vacated the larger house, which they were living in, and turned it over to the church. The couple then moved into the little house.

It wasn't long before Emmanuel and all of the other entities spoke again. "You are coming along very well in your spiritual growth," one said. "You have two cars. You drive the blue one (the smaller and older one) and give the other to us (the church members).

A short time passed, and Emmanuel directed them once again. "Since you are now one with the church," Emmanuel said, "turn over your money to us. We will pay you a salary which will take care of all your food bills. We will pay all of your other bills."

The couple obeyed. They turned over all their money and lived on a small salary, sufficient only to purchase their food and a few necessities. But then things became critical. The church members who had taken their money did not pay the bills. Creditors began to call.

One Saturday morning, the couple talked it over and they realized what fools they had been. They realized the church members had been using them; had in truth been lying to them. They had not paid their bills, and now their home was up for sale to satisfy the payments.

The couple telephoned some longtime friends and told them what they had done and explained their problem. The friends were able to back a loan for them so that they could pay their bills and get their house off the market.

This story came to me in a letter written to me by the couple. They were not ECKists at the time, but they wanted to share what they had learned. The letter ended with "We're older and wiser!" The experience they had had was richer than any response I could have given. My advice is when you step onto a spiritual path, keep your hand on your wallet.

50. God Is Not a Lost-and-Found Department

There was a radio talk show which focused on religion and its meaning to the individual. People would call in to the station and share their viewpoints over the airwaves. One woman called in and reported that her religion worked for her.

"In what way?" the radio host asked.

"One day I lost my very expensive diamond ring," the caller began. "I prayed to Saint Anthony to help me, and I got it back. I lost it a second time and again prayed to Saint Anthony. Once again, it was returned to me. Four times I lost the ring, and four times I got it back."

If we want God to be a lost-and-found person, then we have made God into our own image, a God of materialism or of the human consciousness. The great SUGMAD never requires an individual's worship. IT is concerned only that Soul return home to IT. SUGMAD is not concerned with finding lost diamonds, yet this woman felt she was gaining the spiritual help she needed.

Many of you are struggling to take one more step into the inner worlds. There is a deep yearning to go back home to that Ocean of Love and Mercy. An ECKist may have diamonds and other expensive possessions, but if they were taken from him or if a choice had to be made, he would rather return to the Ocean of Love and Mercy,

SUGMAD, than to keep them. This is the true experience of Soul.

Contemplations...

There is a step beyond prophecy, and this is the spiritual element of the works of ECK, and that is living in the moment.

* * *

Prayer is fine when it is used in its rightful way, and that is to pray for our own spiritual unfoldment. Too often it is used in another way— to control another person.

* * *

If the powers of darkness are thrown against you, then you must put your full attention on the Mahanta and chant HU.

* * *

See a shining light around you through which no evil can come.

* * *

Ask yourself, "What in my emotions has opened the door for this power to attack me?"

* * *

127

Guilt and fear stand between us and our true spiritual heritage.

*   *   *

We must be careful and guard ourselves against those who say they wish to help us in our spiritual life.

*   *   *

You will find this declaration useful as a protection:

I declare myself a vehicle for the SUGMAD.

Wait a brief moment while you feel the certain stream of SUGMAD enter your being.

I declare myself a vehicle for the SUGMAD and the ECK.

And then wait a moment until this flow of ECK fills Soul.

I declare myself a vehicle for the SUGMAD, the ECK, and the Mahanta.

Then go forth to meet your day with confidence, because the Mahanta is always with you.

The hiker found the shepherd and saw that the man was poking holes in the ground with a long stick. Then he dropped an acorn into each hole...

Chapter Six

Goals

51. The Acorn Planter

At the turn of the century a young man went hiking into the outer regions of France. The land was barren and desolate there, but he kept on going, until finally he realized he had gone too far. The water he had brought with him was gone. He knew he couldn't make it back without any water, so he continued walking in the direction he had been going.

After several days, he saw trees in the distance. He felt that his eyes were deceiving him, but he kept making his way closer until he was indeed sure that he did see trees. They were small, but they were there nonetheless, and there were sheep as well. Then he saw a man. He hurried towards him.

The man took him into a small but well-built home, gave him water and food, and told him he could stay the night.

The hiker wondered how the man could survive, alone with his sheep. From the cot where he was resting, he could see the shepherd sitting at the table across the room. In front of him was a stack of acorns. He was lifting them one by one, examining each carefully, separating them into two piles. It was obvious that one stack contained the good ones and the other those which he rejected. Those he rejected, he threw into the fireplace. The others, he carefully put into a little bag. He didn't say a word.

The next morning the shepherd went outside. The hiker stayed behind in the house. When finally his curiosity got the best of him, he went out and looked for the man. After awhile the hiker found the shepherd and saw that the man was poking holes in the ground with a long stick. Then he dropped an acorn into each hole. He would set one and then go a bit further and set another, and so on.

"What are you doing?" the hiker asked.

The man looked up at the hiker as though he had expected to see him there. "Planting acorns," he said. "Out of the one hundred I am planting, probably fifty won't germinate. Of the ones that do, probably twenty-five will be destroyed by insects and several others will be blemished. Out of these hundred, probably ten or fifteen will grow into good trees."

The hiker looked around and saw the small forest he had spotted when he first arrived. It seemed so small in this vast environment and so out of place. He could not help but think how foolish the man was.

Some days later, using the provisions the shepherd had given him, the hiker returned to his home in the city. World War I broke out, and he entered the army to fight the war. When it was over, he felt the need for a little quiet and peace of mind. He remembered the man living in the wilderness, so he set off to find him.

He gradually found his way across the rugged terrain, but when he arrived he almost didn't recognize the place. Where he had once seen the small oak grove, a huge forest now stood. Tall trees were growing everywhere. He hesitated, astounded at what he saw. He thought back to something he had read on the history of the area, recalling that it was said that when the Romans moved into France, the land was fertile. Years ago, fishing artifacts had been found in dry streambeds, evidence that this had once been a thriving area. Other remains of the people who had lived nearby also had been found.

The land was again alive. Now, with the presence of trees, the springs began to well up, and with them came weeds and flowers. And with the flowers, there were bees, and the bees cross-pollinated the whole area.

The hiker spent some time with the man who had planted the forest, and then, in a few days, he returned again to the city.

A few more years passed before the hiker returned to the forest. This time the trees were huge. He learned that men had come into the area and tried to log for fuel, but that it was too far inland and not economical. The man who lived there seemed unconcerned and spent most of his time at the other end of the huge forest planting trees. Every day he went out and planted one hundred acorns.

There was now a village only a couple of miles away. Young couples moved up from the coast. The place had grown so much that the hiker barely recognized it.

He searched for the acorn planter and found him at the far edge of the forest. The man was now old, in his eighties, although he had a youthful sparkle about him. He recognized the hiker and smiled in greeting.

"You have devoted your whole life to planting trees," the hiker said in astonishment, motioning to the forest. "How are you going to enjoy the fruits of your labor?"

The old man looked at the younger man. His expression was unchanged. "It doesn't matter," he answered. "I'm just planting trees. I am enjoying the trees right now, and I enjoy the work."

A year or two later, the scientists visited the forest. They could not understand how the forest had sprung up over the past fifty years. First there was no forest, and then all of a sudden there was a forest. It was a phenomenon to them. They never found the acorn planter. He was off at the other end of the forest with his rod, poking holes in the soil, planting trees.

Then later, the government sent forest rangers to protect the forest. They eventually found the old man's house. Since it was obvious he had been there such a long time, they allowed him to stay, but told him that he was not to light any fires; that it was their job to protect the forest.

The old man didn't argue. He wasn't attached to the forest. It wasn't his.

It so happened that the hiker was a close friend of the forest ranger. He told him the story of how the forest came into being. The ranger then understood and allowed the old man the freedom to do whatever he wanted.

Handing someone a book on ECK is like the man planting acorns. Like him, we are not interested in social changes, but only that the opportunity to learn about the SUGMAD is given to each Soul that is ready.

52. The Right Exposure

When I worked as a cameraman in the print-ing department for ECKANKAR, somebody would bring a job to me. I would take it to the huge printing camera and decide how I was going to most quickly handle it. When I was sharp, I remembered to say, *I am doing this in the name of the SUGMAD;* and I would do it with every bit of skill, love, and attention that I could. But when too many rush jobs were brought to me, a funny thing would happen. I'd slip over the line. I was tired and I would forget. I would be doing the job as a favor for another person.

Doing a job as a favor for another person changed things. All of a sudden the camera didn't work. I'd put the film negative into the developer, and for some reason the exposure was wrong. The whole procedure of developing it and checking it under light would take three or four minutes — from the developer to the water, then over to the fixer, and then rinse and check it on the light table. I was doing this under a red light, under limited light conditions. And then I'd say to myself, "Oh no! Gotta do it over." So I'd run back to throw another piece of film in the camera, adjust the exposures, and try it again. After the second or third miss, when I had used up ten or fifteen minutes and no longer had time to spare, it would occur to me that the reason things weren't working out was because I was trying to do the job for a person. I wasn't doing it in the name of the SUGMAD, in the name of God.

As soon as I realized this, I'd talk with myself: "All right, now you have been hurrying and where has it gotten you? It's been fifteen minutes, and there is nothing to show for it but aggravation. Why don't you just stop, think, and do it right. Do it in the name of God."

It always made a difference, and I know you'll find this true as well.

53. A Custom-Tailored Suit

A salesman had a track record of failure. He had worked for many different companies, but he could never sell their products. So he went from job to job, feeling dissatisfied with himself. Finally, the man became determined to break through the problem. With this attitude he was hired by an insurance company as an insurance salesman.

The sales manager welcomed the new salesman and introduced him to the other members of the sales force. Then he said, "We're in the middle of a sales contest. I'm not going to put you in it because the contest is halfway through, and the man who won it for the past several years is already way ahead. He will probably win again."

The man, who was seemingly a born loser, who had just been newly hired, took the challenge. He was willing to take the extra step and face a challenge which he had never been able to face before in his whole life. "Listen," he said to the sales manager, "I'd like to be a part of the contest. I know I can do it."

The sales manager studied the man. He didn't want to have his new salesman discouraged in a losing race. The other salespeople were already hyped up to sell, sell, sell. They were thriving on positive thinking and trained to keep it up. Still, he couldn't discourage his new salesman by saying no. "All right," the manager agreed.

The new salesman went home. He sat down with a piece of paper and evaluated every job in his past that related to selling. He wrote down every one of his techniques. He put it down on paper and studied the situation. All right, he said to himself, I've done this and this and this. They didn't work. What I am going to do now is something entirely different. And he did it. He set up a whole new sales presentation for himself.

One of the things he came up with was his initial greeting. In the past, when he walked into a client's home, he got right to the point. Now, he moved slowly. He walked in and began talking about the picture on the wall or complimented the clients on their manner of dress and so forth. He spoke casually until the people felt comfortable with him. Gradually, he got into the sales part of his visit.

It worked. The new salesman actually won the company contest. The prize wasn't anything so special. It was a new suit, a custom-tailored suit. He wore it for years, as long as he could. When it was finally worn out, he hung it in his closet as a reminder that there is always one more step. He had learned that there is a way, within our own resources, to find success.

He did it. You can do it too. The Spiritual Exercises of ECK open you up to inner awareness so that you can gain insight into what you are doing in order to do it better.

54. The Independent Merchant

There was a Korean who came to this country to begin a new life. He attended college and received a degree in drama. He tried a number of ways to earn a living and finally went to work for someone who sold produce. He found himself working twelve hours a day. There seemed to be no end to it. The pace was always the same, and he was always tired. He and his family lived in a small one-room apartment for $120 a month. They had no extra money for clothes, except for an occasional pair of shoes.

One day he and his wife made the decision to go into business for themselves. They found a small burned-out shell of a store in Harlem. Instead of trusting vendors to supply the produce, he went to the farmer's market and picked out the fruit and vegetables himself. He now worked eighteen hours a day. For four years he worked without a vacation.

Very slowly, he pieced together a good business. He carried quality produce, and his prices were similar to the supermarket chain down the street. He was willing to work and to work hard. It was different working for himself than it was working for someone else. Working eighteen hours a day for himself never made him tired, whereas working twelve hours a day for someone else had always exhausted him. He saw the important distinction between working for someone else and self-mastery. His life was an example of the freedom he felt, and he was willing to work hard to maintain it.

One of the great lessons this man learned was self-discipline. When he began his business, he was a heavy smoker and always had a pack of cigarettes at hand. One day he realized that the price of cigarettes was cutting into the money he needed to make the business run. He decided that if he didn't have enough self-discipline to stop smoking, he would never have enough discipline to make the business a success. He quit smoking. Any profits were thrown right back into the business. Finally, after four years, he was able to close the store on Sunday and enjoy a little free time.

55. Message to Garcia

During the Spanish-American War, President McKinley wanted to get a message into Cuba to General Garcia who was the leader of the insurgents. He asked one of his aides how this could be accomplished.

"We can't reach him by telegraph nor by mail," the aide answered thoughtfully, "but if it is humanly possible, there is one man who can get a message to him. His name is Rowan."

Lieutenant Andrew S. Rowan agreed to the task and was given a letter from President McKinley for General Garcia. He put the letter in an oilskin pouch and tied it over his heart for safekeeping. Then he set sail in a small open boat.

Four days later, Rowan landed in Cuba. It was night. Moving quickly, he slipped into the Cuban jungle. It was almost as if he had disappeared, because no one reported seeing him for over two weeks, until finally he came out on the other side. It was then a boat picked him up and brought him back to America. He had delivered his message.

Imagine the hardships Rowan had faced. He had achieved success through an understanding of the Law of Attitudes. He knew there was a way, and he carried with him this corrected set of images that allowed for success. He carried the message to Garcia.

56. Paul Twitchell as Writer

Paul Twitchell had an interesting way of putting his talks together and his writings. He would take out a sheet of paper. The first thing he did was to put a title at the top. Then he would put down a string of numbers for the chapters—one to twelve. Later, he would fill in the chapter titles as they came to him. He had the title for the book, and he had the chapter titles. Next, he would fill in the little spaces underneath the chapter title.

Paul set a goal. And when you set a goal, you are placing yourself in a ballpark. Then as soon as you have attained one goal, you can set another. It was in this way that Paul progressed himself through his talks and writings.

Contemplations...

What we are looking for is to achieve the Kingdom of Heaven while we are in the physical body, which means the state of high awareness, or God Consciousness.

* * *

To become a conscious vehicle, or channel, for God, requires that you become the very best that you can possibly be, no matter what you choose to do.

* * *

Build. Act in an uplifting manner, and the Law of Life will never repay you in a negative way.

* * *

You do what you can to make your life right, and when you have done a hundred percent of everything you can do, then Spirit steps in to help with the miracle.

* * *

ECK is the path of doing, of personal experience.

* * *

147

If you are going to do something, don't rush. Start out in time, and if you start out late because you forgot, get there in the natural cycle of things and finish the cycle.

*   *   *

As long as you do not align your actions with your dreams, you are not fulfilling your destiny, because if you can dream something, you can do it.

The lady removed one decanter from the display. The Dream Master took it from her and poured the liquid into some nearby potted plants.

Chapter Seven

Health

57. The Decanter of Sugar Water

One night, while sleeping, a woman walked into a shopping complex with the Mahanta, also known as the Dream Master. She went up the stairs in a department store and stopped before a display of glass decanters offered for sale. They were filled with colored sugar-water to make them more attractive.

The lady removed one decanter from the display. The Dream Master took it from her, and so the contents wouldn't spill, he poured the liquid into some nearby potted plants. After that, they went downstairs to the check-out counter where the manager and salesclerks were standing. The manager was dressed in a very impressive tuxedo and the salesclerks were all in very fine clothing.

"I would like to purchase this decanter," the woman said, handing it to the clerk to wrap.

"What did you do with the liquid?" the clerk asked, examining it.

"I dumped it in the potted plants upstairs," the Dream Master answered for the woman.

The manager was suddenly upset. He told them that their actions were not in keeping with store policy. He reminded them that his store was high class. Then he ran upstairs. Several clerks ran after him. They wanted to see if the woman and the Dream Master had done any damage by dumping the colored sugar-water. Finally, they came back downstairs and said that everything was all right.

153

The Dream Master stood there while the woman paid for the decanter; then the woman woke up.

The lady lay still in bed for a few moments, recalling details of the dream. She understood what the dream meant for her. She knew that sugar was bad for her, and this was reaffirmed by the Dream Master who emptied it from the decanter before she purchased it. She also realized that the thing that was bad for her, the sugar, had a certain degree of respectability in the so-called high-class department store where she shopped. She could see the fallacy and the illusion of marketing tactics.

Time and again, the woman had learned that sugar was bad for her. She had been having health problems connected with it. Until now, she had rationalized that it couldn't be that bad and still be acceptable in society. Now she knew!

If you learn how to work with the Dream Master, you can have a healer in your house, on call every night. You can have a prophet, someone to tell you the future. This is how the Inner Master works. Truth is often taught in the dream state, and it will come mostly in a world we largely recognize, rather than in clouds or floating ethereal places.

58. A Nudge from the Master

A woman came up to me in New Zealand and said that she had a great deal of congestion in her head. When she spoke, she sounded stuffed up, like someone who had a head cold, only it wasn't that at all.

Generally, I don't make comments to people about their health, but every so often I throw something out sideways and see if they catch it.

"Have you had any dairy products lately, while in New Zealand?" I asked.

"Oh yes," she answered. "Just wonderful! Just wonderful!"

"I have heard that dairy products can cause congestion," I said.

"That can't be the problem," she said, "because we live on a farm and I always eat a lot a dairy products."

Unknowingly, the lady had built up her tolerance to a certain level. Combined with traveling, her body became out of balance and suddenly there was a problem. She could have ended it by not eating dairy products for a few days, but she was so sure that she knew what was best that she didn't listen.

I mentioned the answer very quickly and then dropped it. I didn't shake her, take her by the shoulders and say, "Hey, if you want to get rid of that problem, stop eating dairy products for a few days." I cannot do that sort of thing, nor do I want to do it. The truth is that when we operate in ignorance of any law—spiritual or physical, whether it be in economics or nutrition—we are going to suffer from it. We like to fool ourselves by believing that our difficulties arise because we are unfolding so quickly spiritually, but this isn't always so.

59. Self-preservation and Healing

There was an American soldier in Vietnam who suffered from combat fatigue as well as an ailment which the Greeks call *bent back,* meaning the person walked around at a forty-five-degree angle. They didn't know how to help him at the regular medical hospitals at the front, so they transferred him to a psychiatric unit.

Shortly after his arrival, the psychiatrist visited him and studied his situation. "I'm going to give you sodium pentothal, and when you wake up," he said to the soldier, "you are going to be cured." And it happened just as the psychiatrist said. When the soldier woke up, he found himself walking around straight, and he was absolutely furious. The first thing he tried to do was to slug the psychiatrist, jumping on him and swinging his fists. The soldier was really upset because, if he was cured, it meant that he would have to go back into combat. His bent back had been his form of self-preservation.

The story is a little like the television series M.A.S.H., where Klinger tries to get himself out of the service by dressing up in women's clothes. There is really nothing wrong with him. He simply uses his behavior as a form of self-preservation.

The point is that when a person asks for a healing for someone else, it may be that that person doesn't want healing. Maybe that sick person is perfectly happy with his illness because it serves some purpose of self-preservation in his mind. Asking that he be healed is a direct violation of his freedom of choice.

We don't know what another person needs or wants, so when someone approaches me for a healing for another individual, I won't interfere. I turn the request over to Spirit. If someone comes to you and wants healing, whether they are an ECKist or not, it is best to suggest that they see a doctor. If that person has already sought medical aid without result or has an incurable disease and is looking for help, then you can suggest that he or she write to the Living ECK Master. I don't do a healing myself, I simply turn the problem over to Spirit.

It is always best to do everything in the name of Spirit so that you don't pick up karma for yourself. Psychic healers don't know this. They take on the karma of the person they are healing. Their physical stamina may be such that they can do this for many, many years without apparent harm to themselves. Then, suddenly, they will come down with a serious illness and not understand that it was the accumulation of karma from all the people that they had helped cure.

60. The Fasting Plot

In the early history of our country there was an American general nicknamed Mad Anthony Wayne. After serving in the American revolution, he was appointed commander of an army in Ohio, which had twice been defeated by the Indians. For two years he trained his troops. Everything was ready for the battle of Fallen Timbers.

But Wayne had learned that the Indians would fast the morning of a battle. Negotiations with the Indians failed when the Indians refused to surrender, and Wayne replied that he too would fight. But he did not specify the day. For three days, the Indians waited, fasting or eating sparingly. When Mad Anthony Wayne did finally go to battle, the Indians were weakened by their fasting and Wayne was victorious.

About fasting: There are several different methods of fasting for the ECKist. 1) A full fast with water only; 2) a partial fast of fruit or one meal a day; or 3) a mental fast, whereby for a full twenty-four-hour period the chela consciously cancels out any negative thought or keeps his attention fully on the Mahanta.

The fast that you choose should be the one that best fits your circumstances. If you are contributing hard physical work, you need food. If you have a health problem, it may not be good for you to do a full fast. Use common sense. Perhaps the mental fast is better for you. Achieve the

159

mental fast by putting your attention on the Mahanta. Another way of doing it is to take every negative thought and visualize yourself throwing it into the ECK stream and watching it disolve.

Contemplations...

This is how we work with Spirit. We try to look at life and find the laughter wherever we can, whenever we can, because laughter is the healer.

* * *

The condition of health that we suffer is actually a tool to raise us another degree in our state of consciousness.

* * *

Spirit will begin to heal only if you are willing to first help yourself.

* * *

When you ask the ECK for healing, you must open your spiritual eyes and ears to watch for and listen to how the Divine Force is bringing about a change for you.

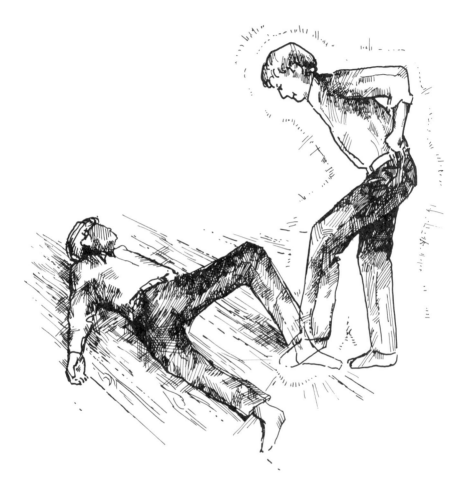

She saw her brother standing on the floor, shaking his leg the way you do when you are taking off a pair of pants and you have one leg free and the other caught in your shoe; only he wasn't taking off his pants...

Chapter Eight

Death/Reincarnation

61. Stepping across the Veil

There was a woman whose brother was very sick. Because he lived several thousand miles away, she wasn't able to be with him physically. She was an ECKist. He was not.

One night she had a strong urge to do a spiritual exercise, so she sat quietly and began her contemplation. Suddenly, she saw her brother. He was standing on the floor, shaking his leg the way you do when you are taking off a pair of pants and you have one leg free and the other caught in your shoe; only he wasn't taking off his pants. The young man was stepping out of his body. He smiled at his sister and said, "Hey, that wasn't half as bad as I thought it would be."

The woman knew that she had seen her brother translate, or die. She had seen him actually stepping across, out of his physical body into the higher spiritual body. She was relieved and happy for him, because she knew he had been afraid. All of his fears had meant nothing. He had moved very naturally into a higher world which was much like this one, only more beautiful and happier and more enjoyable. He was in much better condition than he had been in his diseased and ravaged body. She was able to speak with him. He was happy and laughing, then he was off wandering around in that other plane.

We can meet our friends and loved ones on the other side. It is possible, if you are ready, and if you have developed yourself spiritually.

62. A Funeral Memory

When I was a little boy of four or five, my grandpa died, and the undertaker came to the house and took the body away. Several days later, the undertaker brought the body back again in a casket which he set up on display in our living room. It was to stay that way overnight until the funeral the next day. I remember standing over the shiny wooden casket, staring down at my grandfather. He was laid out in his best suit. Rouge had been rubbed on his cheeks to make him look as alive as possible.

The next morning all of our friends and neighbors stopped by the house. The first thing they did was to go to the casket to see Grandpa. "What a fine job the undertaker did," everyone said. "He appears to be sleeping." From where I stood as a small boy, I watched, thinking that no one made any sense. Grandpa was stone dead. He didn't look real at all.

When the time came for the funeral, the undertaker loaded the casket into the hearse and drove it to the church. It was all very smoothly done. Some men helped carry the casket, almost running down the aisle to the front of the church where another group of people were hurrying around. They opened the casket, next everyone filed past to get a good look, and then they hurried back to their seats crying.

I have cried at funerals. When a loved one leaves us, it is natural to cry. After all, we will miss them. But it is not necessary to cry for the one who has died. The attitude of being sad for the one who dies is a misunderstanding about the nature of Soul. The Bible teaches us that Soul is eternal, but actually Soul is a *being* that is beyond eternity, because eternity is locked into time and space, and Soul is beyond it. This means that Soul is free. So to cry at funerals is not to cry for the departed Soul, but to cry for ourselves.

63. Importance of Self-Realization

There was a man who trusted and followed Spirit throughout his whole life. One time his inner voice told him to sell his business and go into the mountains to start a peach farm. He did it despite all the warnings from his friends who believed him an utter fool. The voice, his inner voice, had told him he would be highly successful.

After working at the peach farm for a number of years, he made a good amount of money and also gained healthful benefits from the fresh air and sunshine. And then the voice came again. "Since you have been here," It said, "you have learned something about construction. Now go into the construction business." And so he did.

There were many in the construction business. The competition was keen, and he didn't do very well. But the voice said, "Build churches." He listened and again trusted the voice. Since none of the other contractors liked to build churches, because of the difficulties of dealing with church building committees, he found this a very profitable line of work. Of course, the church building committees moved slowly, making decisions and then reversing them, but this man was an easygoing individual, astute and mentally sharp. He liked people and communicated well. Consequently, he did well in a field of construction which nobody else wanted. And so, within several years, he became a millionaire. He had everything a man could want—family, a good home, wealth—but there was always a shadow.

As time went on, he became sick with a terminal illness. He found ways of arresting it for a while, using one kind of health treatment after another, but after ten years or so, it was evident he was going to die. As he neared death, he became terrified. Death was something he did not know how to face, and it appeared that his illness would cause him to experience it slowly. As he lay dying, day after day, his fear grew. He began to think of a way out of his terror, remembering that he had a gun in the house. One day he loaded it and put it by his bedside. Lying there, he began to think that he and his wife should die together, and he imagined himself taking both of their lives because he was afraid of going alone.

Although this was a man with faith in Spirit, he was a person afraid, who didn't understand the continuity of life. That is why it is necessary for us to do more than trust Spirit. It is necessary to be aware of oneself as Soul.

64. The Reappearing Kittens

A little girl read a story in *The Wind of Change* about how Zsa Zsa, the cat I had as a boy, died or translated. She wondered how I had felt.

"Well, I felt bad about it," I answered.

She nodded that she understood, then told me how sad she felt when her cat died, but that she realized Soul didn't die. She figured that even though her cat had left that body, it would come back later in another one.

"We used to have kittens on our farm when I was a boy," I told her. "There would always be three kittens about every four or five years. There always seemed to be one gray-and-white kitten, one black-and-white kitten, and one tiger cat. Life was hard on the farm, so they usually translated (died) within a couple of years. But it seemed that all of a sudden we would have the same little group of kittens coming back.

"Soul took a body form," I said, "and when that body wore out, It would leave and come back in a new one. I guess the cats liked our farm because we had so many mice. It was easy to tell that they were the same cats being born again. I recognized my little friends. The same is true when human friends or a member of the family dies," I concluded. "We recognize them when we see them again."

65. Glimpses of the Past

A young girl was taken to a retirement home by her father so that she could visit her great aunt. When they arrived at her room, they met the elderly woman's roommate for the first time. Her name was Sophie. She was well up in years and close enough to the other side that she was getting glimpses of what life was like on the other planes. When she spoke about it, I imagine people said, "Yeah, poor old Sophie. Her mind is going."

The little girl walked into the room, passed her great aunt, and headed straight for the old woman who was supposedly senile. They looked at each other for a long moment. "I know you," Sophie said softly to the little girl, finally breaking the silence. "I knew you when you were an old lady."

The little girl continued staring at the old woman. The look on her face said she was remembering something. "I knew you when you were a young lady," the little girl said suddenly, as though recognizing her.

The great aunt hurried across the room and patted her niece. "Don't mind Sophie," she said lightly. "She is getting a little senile."

It is easy to discredit age and the fantasy of youth when one doesn't have knowledge of the spiritual worlds.

66. Vajra Manjushri

In 700 B.C., there was an ECK Master by the name of Vajra Manjushri who tried to bring the teachings of ECKANKAR to the Persians under King Hakhamanish. The people were steeped in the human consciousness, conscious only of their human form. Vajra Manjushri saw that Soul had gone as far as It could in that state of consciousness, so he tried to raise the consciousness into the spiritual worlds. He was arrested for his efforts.

The authorities strapped him to a huge block of wood, which was shaped in the form of an E. The king's archers formed a line in front of him, shooting their arrows and killing him. The Master's body was then placed in a cave. Several days later, Vajra Manjushri's disciples visited the burial spot, and, like the Christian story, they found that the body was gone.

The disciples began to argue among themselves, mistrusting each other, bickering and accusing each other of removing the body. Just then the ECK Master appeared in a shimmering cloak of light. "Why are you fighting among yourselves?" the Master asked. "The body is merely a clay temple to house Soul. We are merely using the body to visit the physical world."

67. Victory Roll: A Pilot's Dream

A pilot, who flew for a commercial airline, discovered that he had a malignant disease. One night he had a dream.

He saw an airplane that was painted red, white, and blue; he was flying in it and yet above it. He saw himself as Soul, observing the scene, as well as participating in it. Suddenly, without warning, the plane went into a dive. As it dashed downward toward the earth, his whole life flashed before his eyes. Then, just when the plane seemed that it should crash into the ground, it pulled up and started to climb. The pilot was greatly relieved and later described this action in his dream as a resurrection. For him, his dream had been an experience in Soul consciousness, and he saw how quick and easy it was to approach the veil of death. And yet life continues. After the plane had pulled up, it did a victory roll before it flew on.

The dreamer called it *resurrection.* His dream had given him more confidence then any religion could offer. In that moment, he had been able to shake his fear because he knew that he would step forth as Soul after the death of the body. He was happy and uplifted. He had seen that death wasn't even as substantial as a curtain and that life continued.

Contemplations...

When you gain power over the fear of death, there is nothing that can hold you back in this life.

* * *

All that a true spiritual teaching can give you is assurance of the eternal nature of Soul, that you are Soul and that you live forever.

The rabbi reached and took a slip, and then quickly popped it into his mouth and swallowed it. "What did you do that for?" the grand inquisitor bellowed. "God made me do it," the rabbi answered.

Chapter Nine

Intuition/Imagination

68. The Divinely Inspired Rabbi

Many years ago, there was a rabbi who had been brought before an inquisition for heresy. The inquisitors questioned him, carefully weighing his answers, using his responses to build their case against him. But the judge, or grand inquisitor, felt uneasy. The rabbi's answers seemed harmless enough, and he couldn't decide whether he should be found guilty of heresy merely because he did not follow the same God as the Catholic church. Then he had a brilliant idea.

"Take two slips of paper," the grand inquisitor said, "and on one write the words *not guilty* and on the other write *guilty*. After you have done this, fold each piece of paper to conceal the verdict; and we will let the rabbi blindly draw one of them, and therefore pick his own fate. In this way," the grand inquisitor concluded, "the rabbi will be judged by his own God."

The rabbi waited, watching as the two inquisitors carried out the judge's orders. He was a sharp man, aware of human nature and also aware that the men preparing the slips of paper wanted him burned at the stake. Intuitively, he knew that both slips bore the word *guilty*, and he wondered how to save himself.

Just then the inquisitor brought the papers to him. "Pick a slip," he told the rabbi.

The rabbi reached and took a slip, and then quickly popped it into his mouth and swallowed it.

"What did you do that for?" the grand inquisitor bellowed.

"God made me do it," the rabbi answered.

"But how will we know now if you are guilty
or innocent?" the judge demanded, eyeing the
man scornfully.

"It is easy," the rabbi said. "Read the other
slip of paper, and you will know that I am the
opposite of what it says."

A brilliant idea! Where did he get it? Sometimes it is necessary to help ourselves, as the rabbi
did, through Divine Imagination.

69. An Architect Guided by Spirit

An architect in business for himself had a staff of four or five others. He trusted his staff, yet as the engineer in charge of all projects which came through the office, it was his job to double-check the calculations of the others. If there was an error, a building could turn out to be unsafe or a bridge could even collapse. So he took his work seriously.

There was one instance where the mathematical calculations seemed correct on a project one of his associates spearheaded, but he couldn't shake the feeling that there was something wrong. He checked the joints of the beams that held the structure. Everything appeared to be exactly right. Still the feeling kept coming to him that he should check the full computations for the project. Finally, he asked to see everything. As it turned out, he discovered that the beams had been stressed more than they would handle and could have caused a tragedy at some time in the future.

The architect learned to trust the nudges of Spirit. It was how the ECK guided him in his daily life. If everything was all right with a project, he could sense it; and if there was an error, he could feel that something was distinctly wrong.

70. The Australian Bushmen and Divine Imagination

The Australian bushmen, or aborigines, are a native people concerned with preserving nature to maintain a balanced life within it. They kill for food only when necessary for personal nourishment, and to do so, they use the creative imagination.

Long ago, the aborigines used the divine faculty of imagination in inventing the boomerang as a means of winning their prey. A bushman would carefully fashion the instrument, then decorate it with paintings of the animal or fowl to be hunted. He went so far as to draw the detail of the prey. If it was a bird, he carefully described in picture form the type of bird he was hunting and how many he intended to catch. In other words, he clearly defined the object of his hunt by drawing pictures of it on his boomerang. By being so direct, he was bound to get the food he needed to bring back to his family. Much of this understanding has been carried forward to the society of the aborigines today.

This is the use of the creative imagination which is the Divine Self within each of us, the God spark, or Soul. When the creative imagination is working in us, then life is happy and right. You wake up in the morning and everything is rainbows and sunshine. This means you are living and operating under the hand of God.

Contemplations...

Intuition is actually Soul speaking to us and giving us the gentle guidance to make our life better.

*   *   *

We think visualization of anything is an empty fantasy, but it's not. We couldn't imagine something unless there was a reality to it.

*   *   *

Imagination is the God spark within you. This is the only gift of God that we can rightly lay claim to in the physical body — the gift of imagination. If you learn how to use the full powers of the imagination and direct those powers toward the spiritual exercises, you will be able to find ways around the blocks set up by the mind.

*   *   *

Be prepared so that you are always at peace inside yourself, so that you feel you are prepared; and know that the answer, or the solution, for every moment in your life is at hand in one way or another. As long as you are patient and look to that Sound and Light, which may come as a gentle nudge, which may come as a feeling, you will be prepared.

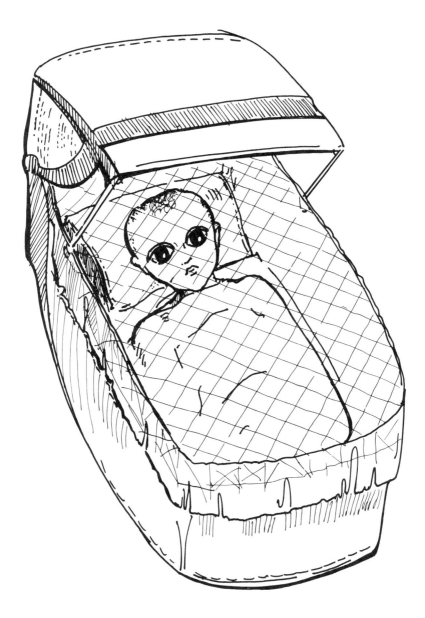

When Truth comes, it is a baby with two big eyes and
it doesn't look at all the way we expect it to...

Chapter Ten

Truth

71. The Ugly Baby

There was a young boy who often wondered if he were adopted. Finally, he got up the courage to ask his mother if it were true.

"No, of course you are not adopted," she told him.

The boy looked at his mother with big round eyes, and he didn't believe her. He had looked through the family album and had seen baby pictures of his older brother, but there were none of him. It stood to reason that there were none because he had once belonged to other parents.

But his mother said, "No, you always belonged to us."

"Then why aren't there any pictures of me?" he asked.

The mother hesitated uncomfortably, then answered, "Because you were such an ugly baby, we were ashamed of you." She paused, having some difficulty explaining, then continued. "When you were a little baby, you were so ugly that all anyone saw when they looked into your crib were two big eyes staring out at them. So, whenever visitors came and asked to see our baby, I told them that you were taking a nap and that I didn't want to awaken you." Then she told the boy how sometimes she'd have him outside in the carriage and would put a blanket over his head so that no one would see him. She had actually kept her son hidden from the world for a number of months.

The boy tried to figure out why his mother thought him so ugly. Then one day, after he had grown up and become a man, his mother handed him a photograph of himself as a baby. Now he knew and understood and agreed that sure enough he had been an ugly baby. The photograph revealed two big eyes staring back.

Today the man still has big eyes, but his face and hair have filled out around them. He is married. One day he told his wife the story of his ugly babyhood.

"Mother found one picture, and I still have it," he said.

"I'd really like to see it," she said.

He went and got it, and showed it to her.

"Oh, what a beautiful baby!" she said. "It looks just like me when I was a baby."

He was startled because no one had ever said anything pleasant about his baby photograph.

This is how we are in regards to truth. When truth comes, it is a baby with two big eyes and it doesn't look at all the way we expect it to. Yet we all pride ourselves that if truth would come, we would instantly recognize it and embrace it. Instead, the prejudices of our narrow human consciousness put a blanket over its head and call it an ugly baby.

72. The Ant Story

My daughter is in grade school. She likes little things, like snails and roly-polies and caterpillars with the fuzzies on them that turn into moths, and she likes ants. Sometimes I tease her, kid her on to a new understanding.

"Do ants have feelings?" I teased. "Little things. They are so small. It makes me wonder if they have feelings." And then I said, "They're like children. They are so small. I wonder if they have feelings?" I said these things to help her grow up.

"Oh, Dad!" she said, aware that I was teasing her.

"Well, suppose the Dad ant," I continued, "who was known to have a great consciousness, explained the way of man to the child ant. He would explain to the child ant that man was a huge thing that thundered past with big earth-shaking steps. The wise father ant would explain to the child ant that, in reality, ants know nothing more than left, right, backward, forward. Suppose he said, 'Someday, we will evolve in consciousness to where we can create great vehicles that will fly us wherever we want to go, all over the world. We will also create something that will record pictures of the past, present, and future.'"

I paused, studying my daughter. I could see that she was thinking about the ant story I had been telling her. Then I continued, "The little child ant looked at the father ant. She knew that her father was supposed to be wise, but what he was saying sounded crazy. 'Gosh Dad,' the child ant blurted out, 'what are you talking about?'

"It is the same way with us," I told my daughter. "Most people see only the world directly about them. They haven't seen what we can evolve to be. We don't ever become God, but we can get the God Consciousness. We can become one with Spirit, and in so doing, we get the God Consciousness. Then we become a Co-worker with God. The ant story explained that there are levels of awareness far beyond us. If I were to talk about them, you wouldn't understand."

73. Abraham's Altar

There are many who follow Jehovah with blind trust. They miss the fallacy of how he is used in Biblical stories, such as the story of the sacrifice of Isaac by his father Abraham, the patriarch of the Old Testament.

Life was good for the people of Abraham. Everything was going smoothly. Then one day, Jot Niranjan, or Jehovah, called down to him and said, "Abraham, I need a sacrifice."

Abraham, who was a good sheepherder, answered, "No problem. I've got a couple of rams around here in pens."

But the Lord God Jehovah said, "No! I have something else in mind this time."

"Anything you want," Abraham said. "Just ask so that I can show that I love, trust, and believe in you."

"All right," Jehovah said, "this time you must sacrifice your son, Isaac."

Abraham was stricken with grief. "Oh no, not Isaac!" he cried out.

The God said something like "I have spoken" and left it at that.

Until this time, Abraham had been left to his own devices. He had even been given the vision of how from his son would come an entire nation, which was to endure the centuries. It didn't make sense. If God wanted him to sacrifice his only son Isaac, then He would be erasing what Abraham had seen in his vision for the future of mankind. Yet, if that was what God wanted, he would do it.

Abraham and two of his manservants loaded wood, which was to be used on the altar, onto a donkey; and then they, along with Isaac, began the three-day journey into the land of Moriah where the sacrifice was to take place.

High in the hills, on the last day's journey, Isaac turned to his father and said, "You know, Dad, we have the firewood, and we can always find stones to build the altar, but we don't have a lamb."

Abraham looked at Isaac. His heart was very heavy with sorrow for the coming loss of his only son, but he said, "Don't worry. The Lord will provide."

Isaac, being a good son, didn't question his father. He believed he was only along for the ride.

Finally, they neared the mountaintop where the sacrifice was to take place. Abraham told the servants to wait, telling them that they would return in a while. Then Abraham walked up the mountain with his son. When they arrived at the summit, they started making the altar.

Isaac, of course, was curious. He looked around but didn't see any kind of offering — no sacrificial lamb, nothing. Then after the altar was finished and all the sticks were laid out around it, his father tied him hand and foot and put him on the altar. Being a good son, Isaac didn't struggle, and he stayed where he was put.

Abraham took the knife and was just about ready to bring it down to end the life of his son, which would have proven his love for and trust in God, when an angel of the Lord appeared and said, "Stop, Abraham! Don't do it! Hold your hand!"

"What for?" Abraham asked.

"Because now I know that you love and trust the Lord." The angel then explained that Abraham had been tested by God.

The fallacy in this story is this. God, who is supposedly omniscient, knows everything, is everywhere, and all-powerful, should have known Abraham was faithful; that his whole heart was with God. It could not have been a test of faith, because God would know.

God does know, doesn't he?

Maybe the highest God knows, but maybe some of the lower gods don't know, and maybe that wasn't the real reason for the test.

Today, we say, "Hey, be careful. Go a little easy on the Biblical stories. There are our patriarchs, you know. The man was trusting in God. Leave well enough alone."

Think about it!

Imagine Abraham living in South Sea Cliff, U.S.A. He wakes up one morning, thinking about the college football game that is going to start at eleven on television, when suddenly the voice of the Lord comes down.

"Abraham!" God called.

"Yes," Abraham answered.

"I want you to go into the backyard, and using the stones left over from your patio, make an altar," God said.

"Yes, Lord," Abraham answered.

"Take your son out there with you," God continued, "and, when the altar is finished, tie him hand and foot and put him on it. Then pour some barbecue lighter fluid on him. I want you to sacrifice your son." And then God goes away.

Abraham is shocked. He loves his son, his only son, who he had hoped would be a college quarterback one day. But he loves and trusts God, so he will do as he was told.

Now imagine that you are the next-door neighbor and you are upstairs in your two-story home. You wake up and you look out the window, a view of your neighbor's patio. To your amazement, you watch as Abraham builds a stone altar. Soon you see him getting out all of his barbecue equipment. He puts wood on top of the altar and then he struggles with his son until he finally ties him up. Then he puts his tied son on top of the altar. What would you do? Do you call the police, or do you pray to God?

Abraham picks up the knife and is ready to plunge it into his son's chest when the Lord stays his hand.

"Hold your hand!" God commands.

Suddenly, the police arrive at the front door. They rush through the house and into the back-yard where they pull their guns ready to fire. "Hold it right there. Drop the knife," one of them yells.

Surprised and embarrassed, Abraham chuckles. "It is all a mistake officers," he says. "God told me to do it, but at the last minute, he said I didn't have to do it. It's okay now. You can go home."

Take a guess.

Where would Abraham end up?

A God who knows everything would not put Abraham in a spot like that to test his faith. We must learn to think and contemplate more on the true meaning of stories which are supposed to relate to truth.

74. Lincoln's Gettysburg Address

Long ago, at Gettysburg, there was held a dedication of the Gettysburg National Cemetery for the soldiers who lost their lives in the Civil War battle that took place there. The keynote speaker was Edward Everett, a renowned orator and candidate for vice president of the United States in the Constitutional Union Party in 1860. As an afterthought, some felt that President Lincoln should be asked to speak as well.

The commissioner in charge of the event at Gettysburg was upset by the suggestion. Lincoln was known to be a rough-spoken man who stood for freedom against slavery, and it didn't appear that he would be reelected. "Do you think he is able to give a talk which is fitting for the occasion?" the commissioner asked.

Edward Everett's talk lasted two hours and he presented it formally, as though he were reading a newspaper aloud, chronicling the events of the battle. When he finished, the crowd greatly applauded him.

Abraham Lincoln was then called to the speaker's platform. He stood hesitantly a moment. His schedule had been so busy he had not had time to write a speech, although he did know the framework of what he wanted to say. He began: "Four score and seven years ago..." and so on. His short speech emphasized that the forefathers of our country had set forth to establish political and religious liberty and that the job was but half finished; that we were now in the middle of the fight to regain and maintain this liberation. When he finished, he quietly stepped down. Those in the crowd were struck by the sincerity of his words, and for a time, there was silence.

Lincoln felt that his talk had been too simple and that he had failed to communicate his message to the people. To his aide, he said, "I should have said more for the men who gave their lives for freedom." All the same, Lincoln's Gettysburg address became one of the key speeches of our country. It has remained an inspiration, a mountaintop for all to look to spiritually.

As individuals, we will, within ourselves, have this Civil War between the positive force and the negative force. It occurs when Spirit (ECK) comes in contact with our human consciousness. Spirit comes in and tries to break up the solidity and rigidness of the mind, so that we are not set in our ways. When our rigidness is broken, we can establish the consciousness of a child to follow the precept: Except that we become as little children, we cannot enter the Kingdom of Heaven. The battle of these forces is a necessary battle that the ECK Masters use to help truth seekers in moving beyond the negative side of their nature to experience the pure, positive God Worlds of ECK.

75. Toad on a Rug

When I arrived in Galveston, it was two o'clock in the morning and I couldn't drive any further. I saw a place that appeared reasonable for twenty-five dollars a night and pulled over.

The man at the desk obviously didn't expect anyone to stop at that late hour, because he jumped a foot off the chair when he saw me. I signed for a room.

The room assigned to me was a shambles. There were no curtains on the windows, and the beds hadn't been made. It appeared that the covers had been pulled up and straightened a little after the last people had left. The armchairs in the room had rips in the center of the cushions, and the bathroom mirror had been ripped off the wall. Right then and there I promised myself that the next night I would find a better place to stay.

The next night I stopped at a place where the room rates started at fifteen dollars a night.

"What kind of room would you like?" the woman at the window asked.

"Well, what do you have?" I asked.

"Fifteen dollars gets you a bed," she answered.

I took the room only to realize that the woman had been exact in her description. I got a bed and an old bathtub, not even a shower. There was a toad in the room too. When I first entered the room, I couldn't find the light switch and it was dark. The toad was sitting camouflaged on an old rug. I almost stepped on him. He hopped off into the bathroom and crawled into a crack under the bathtub. That was when I spotted a big hole in the wall. I had half a mind to go back to the desk and tell them that this was absolutely the worst motel I had ever stayed in in my life, but I decided not to do it. Instead, when I went to bed that night, I shut the bathroom door so that the toad couldn't get into the room while I slept.

The next morning, I stopped by the front desk. A young woman brushed passed me. "Is the hot water fixed yet?" she called out.

The manager looked up from his desk and smiled. "They are working on it right now. It ought to be fixed any minute," he said politely.

"This is Thursday," she said again. "I have been here since Monday, and there still isn't any hot water."

I listened, suspecting that management hadn't furnished any hot water for a couple of years and didn't intend to get any. What did it matter? If one tourist left, another would stay because it was cheap. The management could keep making money without the high cost of heating water. The woman, who had been there since Monday, stayed like a helpless sheep.

The next day, I arrived at my destination. In comparison, the hotel there was like a palace.

We put ourselves through experiences, such as cheap motels, so that we appreciate more of what we have. I do this sometimes too, and sometimes I do it because I travel later than I should and it becomes the only lodging available. It doesn't matter as long as we can see the humor in it.

76. Satan: Secret Agent of God

A nine-year-old girl went to her father and said, "There is something wrong about the story of God, the Devil, and hell."

The father put down his newspaper and studied his child. "What do you mean?" he asked.

"Well," the little girl said hesitantly, "God loves good people, doesn't he?"

"Yes," the father said.

"And the Devil favors the bad people, doesn't he?" she asked.

"That's true," the father answered, realizing his daughter was leading him somewhere.

"So the good people that God loves go to heaven, and they enjoy all kinds of good things there," the little girl said.

"That's right," the father said.

"But the Devil," the little girl said, "the people who like him, they go to hell for a reward. Then the Devil punishes them and puts them in fire and eternal damnation."

"Yes, that's true," the father said, nodding his head.

"It doesn't make any sense," the little girl said. "It would make more sense if the Devil would treat those in hell very nicely for having served his purpose."

The father stared at his daughter. He didn't know what to say.

The little girl had decided that the Devil was actually a secret agent for God. It was his task, she

decided, to test people on the principles of God by
finding out if they understood them. She had
more insight than the clergy who preach that
Satan is a totally negative being, who somehow is
able to continue working in this world. She asked
why, if Satan wasn't an agent, God wouldn't
squash Satan like he was some kind of bother-
some bug. She knew that Satan had a very good
purpose on earth. She was right. His purpose is to
put Soul to the tests and trials that are necessary
for It to come into a realization of Its Godhood.
Satan is the negative power which we call Kal.
This negative force is a working part of the Divine
Plan.

77. A Coin Trick

There was an individual I knew who performed an excellent coin trick. He would hold a coin in his hand, show it to you, and say, "Now here it is in my left hand. I'll put some whiffle powder on it and see what happens." He sprinkles the imaginary powder with his other hand and then quickly claps his hands. The coin is gone. Then, when you were completely mystified, he'd reach into his pocket or behind your ear and come up with the coin and say, "Well, for heaven's sakes, here it is. I don't know how it got there. It must have slipped in from somewhere."

To most people there would be no objection to this magician's trick, but one day he happened to perform it for a person who belonged to one of the fundamental churches. The person was very gullible about things and he knew it, so he explained first. "I am going to do a trick and it is only a trick," he said, so that there would be no misunderstanding.

Suddenly, he made the coin disappear. The woman's eyes went as big as the coin, and she yelled, "Demonology!"

The magician was shocked. "No, it is only a trick," he assured her. "I can't explain it to you because it is a secret of the trade."

The woman and her husband finally relaxed and said that they understood and that they realized it was a trick. But an interesting thing happened. They had been renting an apartment from the magician for some time. Two weeks after the coin trick, without explanation, they moved out.

The lesson in this story is this: You don't always know another person's state of consciousness, even when you are talking about the ECK to them. To some, when you try to explain Soul Travel, they will hear astral travel or mind travel, or something which sounds like the workings of the devil. This is an attitude that is established in their minds, either from this lifetime or another, and there is no hope for them. The only protection you have is to steer clear. Keep away from people of this sort of consciousness. They resist truth. They would rather die than yield to it.

Truth is like a camel walking up to us in the desert. The person who is thirsting for truth but doesn't recognize it when he sees it, throws a stone or a stick at the camel, and so, he loses out.

Contemplations...

When you ask God, "Please show me truth," and you haven't used your talents today, you can't expect to find the greater talents, the greater truth tomorrow.

* * *

For the freedom of Soul, this is the sequence that must occur: Purification of the mind and then comes liberation of Soul. You have to have one, then the other.

* * *

SUGMAD really doesn't care about a person's individual problems. All SUGMAD cares about is that one day Soul will become ITS Co-worker, because Soul is required by God to see, realize, and recognize Its own worlds.

* * *

Life is a mystery until we come to the path of ECK and begin to come to the understanding that we can be the creators of our own world.

* * *

The Law of Silence means not to wear our troubles on our shirt sleeve where other people can look at them and discuss them.

* * *

Soul is the essence of God. Soul is not God, could never be God. We can never be one with God, although we can be one with Spirit.

* * *

The secret teaching which we speak of in ECKANKAR is secret only because we haven't found the source within ourselves, or the key to unlock it.

* * *

All our beliefs are valid and, in truth, there is no right or wrong. There is only the state of consciousness where we are now.

* * *

When you ask for truth and your heart is pure, Divine Spirit will take you one step closer home to God.

* * *

The principles of Spirit are embedded in the literature and in the life of our culture. They are there. Truth is never hidden. It is always available for the Soul who wants to take the next step.

"I know there is an Inner Master," she said. "But, what will I do with my guardian angel?"

Chapter Eleven

Inner and
Outer Masters

78. Guardian Angel

One evening, a lady in the audience stood up to make a statement and to ask a question.

"I know that there is an Inner Master," she said. "And I know that at the time of death this Inner Master will come and escort me across the borders of death into a land that is prettier and happier than earth. But," she said, loudly, pausing, shifting uncomfortably from foot to foot, "what will I do with my guardian angel?"

"What do you mean your guardian angel?" I asked.

"Ever since I can remember," she said, "I have had this guardian angel, a man in long, flowing robes. The reason I am here tonight is because he told me to come. He said that ECK was the next step in my spiritual unfoldment." She let out a sigh and raised her arms up to the ceiling, palms up, motioning that here she was, taking the next step.

This lady provided an interesting experience for the rest of the people in the audience. I had been trying to give them knowledge of the Inner Master, and the lady in the audience demonstrated it.

"What do I do with my guardian angel once he transfers me to the ECK Masters?" the lady asked again.

"Don't worry about him," I answered. Then I explained that her guardian angel would now probably work with someone else and that she didn't have to worry about him anymore. I explained that consciousness, whether it reveals itself as the Christ Consciousness, the Mahanta Consciousness, or any other state of consciousness, is merely a form through which the Holy Spirit, or the ECK, forms a matrix, a mold to reach each person at his own level.

79. Spiritual Masters Are People Too

At an ECK campout, I was throwing a softball with Bruce, who I had played with on the office team a few years back. It felt good throwing the ball again. I was throwing wild, but there was plenty of open space behind him.

"No problem," Bruce said, knowing that he was a good catcher.

Then I became real adventuresome, and I started to throw with the other hand. The ball got away from me and flew off into the bushes.

Bruce rushed to the edge of the bushes and stood there, looking around until I arrived. It was then that we discovered the creek, and the ball was in it.

Everybody wanted to help. One person came up with a little broom, but it didn't quite reach the ball. Then someone had the idea that if they made a mudball and threw it on the other side of the softball, bouncing it, the ball would work free. And it did.

Later, Bruce and I were throwing the ball again. This time others had joined us, and we got to talking. "You know," I said, laughing, "in the old days, a man of God would walk quietly down the road with his head bent in prayer. He'd go into a little town with such reverence that the people there knew the man was a spiritual master.

"And now, look at me. Really, what must people think? I can imagine them saying something like 'You know the guy's out there and he throws a softball that ends up in the creek. What kind of a spiritual master is that?'"

80. The Accused Juror

An ECKist had been called to jury duty, and so she went to the place where the other jurors were waiting to be called into court. She sat quietly, minding her own business, when another juror came over and sat down in the seat next to her.

"Do you go to church?" the woman asked out of the blue.

"No," the ECKist answered, without explanation.

The woman's eyes narrowed upon her. "Well, you are going to hell then," she said, and she went on and on about being saved from the devil, etc.

The ECKist was amazed at the outburst but remained detached. Everyone turned to look at her. Instead of reacting, she looked to the Inner Master and silently chanted HU. There would have been a time in her life when she would have been embarrassed by this woman, but she wasn't now. Now she merely looked upon the woman's outburst as another Soul trying desperately to prove to Itself that Its religion was righteous, because It obviously didn't feel that It was.

You will find that when someone is pressing his faith upon you, it is because he is not very sure of it.

81. A Beggar in Disguise

A university student in Europe had finished an evening class and was on his way home. He quickly hurried to the tram station and waited for his ride. As he was waiting, a man dressed as a beggar came up to him and shook his hand. The student was surprised and could not take his eyes off the man. He looked like a beggar, but then again he didn't. His eyes were clear and glittering, and his face was kind and gentle.

They began conversing. The beggar told him that he was waiting for his ship to leave the next morning and that he needed a little money to tide him over for the night.

All of a sudden, the tram arrived. "Excuse me," the student said, abruptly, "my tram is here. I gotta go." As he ran off to get the tram, he heard the beggar say in a sad tone of voice: "Yes, Eric, go on. Catch your tram."

As the student left on the tram, he began wondering about the beggar. Later it dawned on him that he had met an ECK Master in disguise.

82. An ECK Miracle

At the 1984 ECKANKAR Creative Arts Festival in Boston, two Higher Initiates in ECK were walking down a hallway, talking about how to be a vehicle for Spirit. As they rounded a corner, they came to a lounge area, and there lying on the sofa was a woman who was in great pain. Two men were standing helplessly on either side of her. It seemed that she had slipped a disc in her back and was unable to move. The people were guests at the hotel but were not ECKists. No one seemed to know what to do because every time they touched the woman, the pain was so great she would cry out.

Quite spontaneously, one ECK Higher Initiate moved in close and looked at the woman lying there. "In the name of the SUGMAD, get up!" she commanded.

And the woman moved. All of a sudden, she got up. She looked at the two women whom she did not know and said, "I don't know what you did, but thank you." And then the two men helped her out the door to get medical assistance for her back.

The two ECKists turned around and walked down the hall. One of them turned to the other and said, "My God, a miracle!"

83. Apprentice to the Mahanta

When we want to learn a trade, we become an apprentice in that trade. If it is experience in the electronics field that we wish, then we seek work with a company that is staffed with excellent engineers. As a new employee, one hopes to be assigned to an individual who is both knowledgeable and who can teach the secrets of electronics. It is better to learn by experience than it is through a book, although if a book is all that is available, the book will provide a beginning.

These same principles apply to our spiritual life. It is necessary that we find someone with experience to teach us. The path to mastership actually requires that we find the ideal, the right teacher to equal the achievement that is sought. This is not found in a teacher's physical presence, because the personality can be misleading. To the Christian who seeks the ultimate in Christianity, this means finding a person who is a channel for the Christ Consciousness. The ECKist looks to the Mahanta, who is the highest consciousness one can look to in the field of ECK.

84. Beetle Bailey Cartoon

One Beetle Bailey cartoon strip showed the sergeant standing there with his left hand around Beetle's throat. He had his right hand in a fist, clenched, drawn back, ready to let Beetle have it.

Beetle didn't resist, his mouth was drawn into a curvy line; and he just stood there. "Beetle," the sergeant growled, "you've been my greatest disappointment."

In the next cartoon frame, the sergeant is still holding Beetle the same way. Beetle wonders what's stopping the sergeant from punching him. "Why can't I make you change?" the disgusted sergeant asked, "Why can't I make you grow?"

Beetle isn't ready to take any of the responsibility himself. "Well, Sergeant," he said, "maybe you just don't have a green thumb."

He threw the whole situation back at the sergeant.

There is a spiritual principle in practically everything. The spiritual principle is in Beetle Bailey cartoons. It is everywhere.

When asking for help from a spiritual master, whoever it is — Jesus, Buddha, Krishna, etc. — it is expected that help will come. Many expect the spiritual masters to do everything for them. Sometimes the master will set certain disciplines for the individual. He will say, "If you want to see the Light of God, do this . . . " The master often gives directions, but the individual is just too lazy to listen to what it is he is saying.

85. Oracle at Delphi

The oracle at Delphi in Greece was once used by people in an attempt to learn what the future held. Others asked it for help of some kind. The oracle itself was underground, attended to by a woman who was the high priestess. When a person came to the temple or to the oracle, he would stand outside for several weeks or months, until one day the high priestess would approach him and say, "All right, the oracle will see you now."

Then the person would descend into the underground room. It was felt that Apollo took over the oracle, and the priestess then spoke with a deep man's voice to give a prophecy. In this particular case, the man seeking help had a very bad case of stuttering, and he walked in wanting a cure.

"You have come for a voice," the oracle said in a loud, booming voice, before the man even said a word.

It was true. The man wanted a voice that would speak without stammering.

"Go to Libya," the oracle's voice boomed again. "Conquer the land and raise flocks, abundant flocks of the different animals that are there."

The man protested. All he wanted was to have his voice so that he could speak the way other people did. But finally, after considering what the oracle had told him, he went to Libya. He got into a battle with the people there, and during the battle he found that he had lost his stammer. After he had conquered the land, he also found that now he had the material goods that he needed to lead the people into a better life.

In a way, the man had asked Spirit, Divine Spirit, or the Holy Spirit, to give him a healing for his voice. The answer had come through the oracle, which said, but first earn it. You have to go out into the world and conquer it through your efforts. Spirit was actually looking out for his well-being in a very broad sense. Not only would he have his voice, but he would also have those things in his life which were good for his spiritual unfoldment.

Contemplations...

The purpose of the Living ECK Master is not to destroy religions, but to enliven them.

*   *   *

Who and what you are doesn't concern me. All that concerns me is that Soul is willing to make Its way back home to God and that It has every opportunity to do so.

*   *   *

When we get secrets from the Inner Master, we keep them to ourselves.

*   *   *

The Living ECK Master has roamed the earth for centuries and has given the opportunity, again and again, to individual Souls who were just about ready to step onto the path of ECK.

*   *   *

All I am offering you is a glimpse of the face of God through personal experiences in the Light and Sound of this Divine Being.

*   *   *

The purpose of life is to give Soul an education so that It can become a Co-worker with God. Whether we like it or not—resist, cry, scream, shout, throw a tantrum like a child—someday we are going to be one of the exalted ones, a master in our own right.

* * *

Self-mastery means simply that a person has the capability of running his own life according to the laws of Spirit. This presumes that you know the laws of Spirit. This understanding comes through the Light and Sound of God directly. It's a direct infusion of the Shariyat-Ki-Sugmad into Soul.

All of a sudden, he heard a buzzing sound. It sounded like the buzzing of a fly...

Chapter Twelve

Initiation

86. A Sound of God

A man who had just received his Fourth Initiation was sitting at his desk in his office. He was trying to study some inventory reports but, at the same time, his mind was on the initiation he had just received. All of a sudden, he heard a buzzing sound. It sounded like a buzzing fly. He raised his head and looked around the office. Because he was a gentle-hearted Soul, he thought that if he could find it, he would help it to go outside. He looked but he couldn't see it.

He rose to his feet and looked about for the fly, listening to feel his way to where the fly was buzzing. It wasn't in his desk. It seemed off to the left, and so he went toward the file cabinet. Believing it was in there, he opened a drawer. He was thinking that the fly would fly out and then he would catch it and carry it outside, but it wasn't in there. He opened the second drawer but it wasn't in there, and then the third and it wasn't in there either. Finally, he put his ear to the file cabinet and decided that it sounded like the buzzing was coming from the fourth drawer. He opened that drawer, but it wasn't in there either.

Somehow, he thought, the fly must have gotten back into one of the other drawers again. He opened them all. He waited and waited. The buzzing continued. He was really puzzled.

All of a sudden another person walked into the office, and, just that fast, the buzzing stopped.

He was real quiet and didn't say much to the person.

Later, he looked up the God Worlds chart in *The Spiritual Notebook*. There it explained that the sound of buzzing came from the Etheric Plane, which is the height of the Mental Plane, or the Fourth Initiation. He understood the connection, that it was the voice of God coming to him in one of the many sound forms It takes.

The Sound can come as thunder or as a flute. It may also come in many other forms, like the chirping of sparrows. It is the sound of the atoms of God moving in the high worlds. When you hear a sound at a particular place or of a particular kind, it means that in Soul Consciousness you are there. He was at the Etheric Plane, and it meant that Spirit was purifying him in a state of being on that plane. It was uplifting him in consciousness, although he didn't recognize it at the time.

87. The Path of Life

A young man went to a master and said, "I want to be your student so that I may find the way to God."

The master looked the young man up and down, studying him. "Well, from the looks of you, it's going to take a great deal of gold to teach you," he said.

"I don't have any gold," the young man said.

"Well, go out and get it," the master answered.

And so the young man went out into the world. He worked hard for a number of years, laboring to earn enough gold to be accepted by the master. Finally, he felt that he had enough and returned to the wise man, placing his earnings at the old man's feet.

The wise old master looked up at the younger man. He saw that he was much older than when he last saw him and that he had labored hard, but all the same he said, "I have no use for this gold, because I have the blessings of God in my lap anytime I want them."

The younger man was astounded and started to argue that he had merely followed the master's instructions, but the old man interrupted him. "If you haven't learned anything from the experiences of life while earning this gold," the wise man said, "then I can teach you nothing."

This is what the path of ECK is about, so go out into life and get your experiences.

88. Thomas Merton's Discovery

Thomas Merton, Catholic mystic and author of *The Seven Storey Mountain*, spent his life struggling and searching for the meaning of God. His goal was to come to some realization and understanding of what God wanted of him.

One day, Merton went outside and lay down on the ground. His cheek rested against the dirt of the earth. "God," he murmured against the earth, "I know what you want of me. You want me to stop thinking so much about myself." (He didn't know that his superior was standing over him, watching and wondering about his behavior.) "No, no, you don't want that of me at all," Merton continued, talking aloud. He was still face down on the ground. "You want me to think more about you." And then he started to laugh out loud. After a moment, he interrupted himself. "No, it isn't even that. You want me to go into the area of consciousness where there is no thought."

Thomas Merton had seen the truth of which Socrates had spoken: "Man, know thyself." When you know yourself, you go beyond the mind. Soul then operates by direct perception. It is a state of consciousness which cannot be explained or defended. All that I can do is to tell you that you can discover it for yourself, through the Spiritual Exercises of ECK.

89. The Lawn Mower

My daughter decided that she wanted to have a lawn in our tiny backyard, which is about the size of a postage stamp. I told her, "Listen, if you want grass, you'll have to be responsible for it. You'll have to cut it." She agreed and we went down to a department store and purchased a small, reel-type push mower for our little patch of grass. My daughter was excited about it and couldn't wait to get to work.

You know how kids are at a young age. They believe everything is made of steel, iron, stone, granite, or what have you. She didn't think about the fact that the little roller at the back of the mower was plastic, so when she dragged it over a concrete step and it broke, she didn't feel responsible. All of a sudden she comes into the house pleased as punch and says, "The lawn mower's broke."

I hesitated before asking her how it happened. Since I had been a kid myself, I knew how things happened. I would usually do something that wasn't supposed to be done. I'd overdo it. "All right," I said finally, staring at her, "how did it break?"

"Oh, I was just mowing the lawn," she said, "and this little brace for the roller on one side broke off." Then she told me about the concrete step and what really happened.

I shook my head, remembering what it was like to be a kid.

"It'll be okay," she said, reassuring me, "I'll get the Elmer's Glue, and I'll fix it. It'll be okay."

Kids of that age believe Elmer's Glue will fix anything.

She went back outside. A while later, I looked out and saw that she had Elmer's Glue smeared all over the back side of the mower where the roller attached. She looked up and saw me. "When it dries, it'll be okay," she said.

I shook my head again and told her we would have to get a new brace for the roller. She offered to pay for it, but when we got to the store, we found that we couldn't just purchase one brace for twenty-five cents, we had to purchase a package of them for a dollar. So I paid.

When we got home with the parts, I decided to give the responsibility back to her again. "Go out into the garage," I told her, "and get two wrenches. You are going to need two wrenches. Then put the new brace in place of the broken one on the mower." I knew she could fix it if she sat down and thought about it.

She went out and got the wrenches and laid them down next to the mower, then she sat there puzzled.

"I'll give you a hint," I called out to her from the doorway.

She looked up at me.

"Put it on the same way as the one that isn't broken," I suggested. "When you get the roller on, put all the spacers in between them."

She took the lawn mower apart. The pieces were scattered all over the backyard. I watched her for a while, wondering how I could impress upon her that if she kept things neat, it would be

246

easier. If she kept things neat, she wouldn't have to hunt for pieces in the radishes and underneath the rosebushes.

A while later she came inside and announced, "It's fixed! Do you want to come out and look?"

"Sure do," I answered. You know, I went outside and saw that she had actually fixed the thing. She was so proud. It was as if now this was her personal lawn mower. It was obvious that she felt that she had helped produce it. She had helped manufacture it, and now she had the pride of ownership.

The Living ECK Master, or the Master power, works in this way. It will let you start fixing things yourself. You start learning how to do things, and you also learn to avoid doing things that hurt you or that cause pain. You look for the things in your life that help you and that will make your life more positive, happy, and provide cheerfulness.

90. A Master and the Baby

A master was walking with several of his disciples. The small group paused before a bungalow where a mother was bringing a newborn infant out into the sun, placing the child on a blanket spread out on the ground. The baby was wiggling its little hands, reaching for its feet, which were kicking in the air, and playfully grabbing at itself and laughing. As the disciples stood there watching, one asked the master, "What is Self-Realization?"

The master walked over to the blanket, lay down beside the baby, and put his feet and hands in the air, gurgling and cooing in imitation of it.

What the master was trying to illustrate, I can't tell you in words. You'll have to experience it. He was saying, as it is said in the Christian Bible, except ye "become as little children, ye shall not enter into the kingdom of heaven."

Self-Realization is the first real step into the Kingdom of Heaven, because it is in the first of the spiritual worlds which lies above the heavens of orthodoxy — Christianity, Buddhism, and the Indian religions.

91. No Room in the Tent

At an ECK campout, I met a little boy walking outside the meeting hall. We walked together and he was talking, telling me he had a scratch on his foot.

"Did you just get that scratch?" I asked him.

"No."

"Had it before, huh?"

"Yeah."

We walked a little further and he stepped on a rock with his bare feet. "Ohhh," he moaned, bending over. "That one got me.

After a moment, we continued walking. A short distance down the path, the little guy paused. "Do you see the tent back there?" he asked, pointing.

I nodded.

"That's where I sleep," he explained. Then he gave me the whole family history. When he finished, he hesitated, looking at his tent. He was deciding if he would invite me to stay. "It's too small," he said finally. "You know, you can't stay."

"Gee, that's too bad," I said, playing along with him. "I was just thinking of asking you if I could stay over tonight."

The little fellow thought about it a while. "Maybe there's room," he said finally.

The little guy is like Soul when It first considers the possibility of God-Realization. It says, "Something so grand can't be for me. There isn't room in my little world for the one who can show me the way to God."

The Master says, "Look again, look again." And Soul awakens to the possibility there may be room in Its consciousness for the Mahanta and God.

92. Preparation for Initiation

When the ECK Master Milarepa was a student on the spiritual path, he and some of the other disciples approached the Master Marpa. "Can we help carry some of the load, Master?" they asked.

The Master Marpa studied the students and then shook his head. "No," he said, "you cannot."

"But please!" Milarepa begged. "Let us carry some of the load for you."

Marpa considered this and finally agreed, but first he drew everyone's attention to a very heavy oak door. He explained that there he would place a small part of the load.

Instantly, the heavy oak door split in two. The disciples looked on, too astonished to speak. And so from that point, they realized that each individual is given or earns his share of the Sound and Light of ECK.

93. The Tunnel

One time, the negative power, known as Jot Niranjan, or Jehovah, returned from a long journey to the outer reaches of his domain. He came home to his banquet hall where all his subjects were feasting. He had been very good to them, giving them all the comforts of life.

The Lord sat down at the banquet table and watched as his people ate. There was something disturbing him. He had been away from his kingdom on the Astral Plane for quite awhile, and now he saw things with fresh eyes. He saw that his subjects had been stealing from him. Jot Niranjan (Jehovah) was upset, but he didn't show it. He just looked up and down the long banquet table, thinking. Everyone was having such a good time eating and drinking his food and wine that no one noticed. Finally, when the meal was over, he said, "I have been observing you, thinking on the fact that all of your comfortable positions in life depend upon how you please Jehovah." He paused, looking at them.

The people suddenly realized that he was displeased with them. They all started trembling, unsure of what to do.

"First, I have taken you in," the Lord said, sounding a warning to them. "I have taken you from the gutters; and I have given you work, plenty of food, clothes, and enough to care for those you love." He paused again then asked, "But what have you done?"

No one in the banquet hall moved.

"It wasn't enough," Jot Niranjan continued, "that I take care of you. You wanted me to take care of your spouses. Okay, I did it. Next, you wanted me to care for your uncles, nephews, aunts, and nieces—those who didn't even reside under your roof. I did that too." He paused. His eyes flared with anger. "But this is too much. Now you want the cats and dogs in here as well, and I don't want it.

"And look at this food," the great Lord Jehovah yelled, motioning to the overabundance on the table. "You have wasted half of it. You know, you would all benefit by going down into the tunnel where the slaughtering is done. You would see how this meat you waste is made. Perhaps you would understand if you had to labor with the slime up to your knees, covered with grease, taking in the smells and the feeling of it."

All the people at the banquet table were sitting very quietly now. They knew they had gotten the old man mad and that the wealth and good fortune they had been enjoying was in jeopardy. However, they were relieved when, finally, Jehovah dismissed them.

Curiously, one person remained behind. After everyone had left, he approached Jehovah, questioning him about the tunnel where all the slaughtering was done. "Is there really such a place?" he asked.

Jot Niranjan (Jehovah) studied his subject and laughed. He showed he could be jovial and happy, not only the vengeful god of the Old Testament. "Yes, there is," the Lord said.

"Where is it?" the man asked.

"The entrance to it is in that storage shed over there," Jot Niranjan said, leading him outside the banquet hall and pointing to a place not far from them. "But it is all jammed up with old junk."

The man followed Jot Niranjan and looked in the direction the Lord was pointing. What he said was true. He could see that the entrance was indeed all jammed up, but still he was curious. He was interested in spiritual unfoldment, not in preserving his wealth and so-called easy life in Jehovah's kingdom. He was thinking that perhaps the tunnel led somewhere. "I would really like to see it," the man said finally.

Again Jot Niranjan studied his subject. The man had been with him on the Astral Plane for quite awhile. He had been a good subject and had led a good life. "Are you sure?" the Lord asked. "That tunnel is like a sewer filled with dirt and scum. You would have to bend over to walk through it; and it is very dark, like a black hole."

"Yes, I really want to see it," the man said again.

Jot Niranjan went over to the hole and removed bags of junk and old trunks from the cover. Then he pulled the cover back. The smell of rotten things was very strong, and it was very dark, but the man with him was very curious about what was down there. He went down into the hole.

Jot Niranjan called after him. "Keep going east," the Lord called. "Keep going east and just keep going. Feel your way along the walls and don't fall down."

The man went along, feeling his way through the tunnel until, gradually, he saw a light, realizing that he was coming to the end. He hurried along and finally stepped out into a brilliantly lit kingdom. It was so bright that, at first, he was blinded, although he knew instantly that he had entered a better and higher world than the one he had left. He knew the tunnel had been an entranceway.

As the man stood on the other side of the tunnel, the voice of Jot Niranjan echoed behind him. "The pearls of wisdom in my kingdom are put where only the humble in station will find them," the Lord's voice sounded. And so, gradually, the man became accustomed to the light, and he saw a kingdom of pearls and diamonds and light and cleanliness. He was now ready to become a resident on this next plane.

Contemplations...

The reason for spiritual enlightenment is not to escape life, but to learn how to live it richly and enjoy it.

* * *

The purpose of the initiation word you use is to create that spiritual foundation where you become so strong, that no matter what comes up, you instantly remember to chant your word. All that you are doing is opening yourself to the full help of Spirit that is around you anyway. What this does is open the floodgates of your understanding.

* * *

One of the principles, or laws, of ECK is that there is always one more step. There is always one more heaven.

* * *

The Light of God dispels ignorance, and the Sound of God carries us home.

* * *

Trust in Spirit to bring you whatever you need for your unfoldment.

* * *

Once you touch the hem of God's garment, you are never the same. One of the biggest changes you find, as you come back to physical consciousness, is that you are the only awakened individual in a world of sleeping people.

* * *

When you become as little children, you shall see the Kingdom of Heaven. You will carry no ideas from the past to hold you, none of the future to frighten you, but just the present, with the assurance that everything you need to know is already at hand—every answer, every solution.

* * *

A person who has a high degree of spiritual unfoldment will be balanced in his everyday life. He will use common sense and common courtesy with the people around him.

* * *

When greater amounts of Light and Sound come in, we must give out a greater service.

* * *

As we go higher and raise ourselves in the spiritual consciousness, we are able to solve the problems of life. We are happy. We are at home in every environment.

* * *

The higher you go in Spirit, the more you expect of yourself, because the Inner Master says to you, "There is always a better way to do it." So It gently nudges you to bring out the best, because this is the preparatory work that is being done for the individual Soul to one day step into God-Realization.

* * *

As we grow in Spirit, we must one day become an adult in the Worlds of God.

* * *

When you get above the Mental Plane, you get to the Soul Plane and you stop Soul Traveling. At this point, you move most often in a condition called seeing, knowing, and being. You simply find yourself on the other plane of spiritual consciousness or in another heaven. You are simply there.

* * *

The difference between initiates is: A First Initiate can see perhaps a small little ring like this, formed by my hands. They can see just a small part of the interrelationship of what happens with people out here, as it connects with the inner. An initiate of the Second Circle sees more. His scope is greater. The higher you go, the more you can see; and the more you can see, the better you are able to arrange your life.

* * *

What you are looking for is to become the conscious Soul, the awakened Soul. This means that you are completely free of outer influences in your life.

* * *

Don't detour from your goal of God-Realization. Keep your eyes on the high aspiration which Soul has taken the trouble to come into the lower worlds to attain.

* * *

When you walk the path of ECK, do it while you embrace life with both arms and with joy. Be not afraid of the sorrows it will bring, but be aware of the love that Spirit is pouring into you. You are now becoming—in your own way, at your own pace—a spiritual giant.

GLOSSARY

AUDIBLE LIFE CURRENT. The Divine Being expressing ITSELF in a ray both audible and visible like a radio wave flowing out from the Supreme Creative center of the Universe of Universes; life force that can be heard and seen with the spiritual vision and objective sight; the all-embracing spiritual force of the SUGMAD, which composes life and makes up all elemental substances including the component parts of Soul; the ECK.

ECK (EHK). The Audible Life Current; all that is life; life force; Holy Spirit; the creator of things; the great forming force which works in a creative way; the essence of SUGMAD.

ECKANKAR (EHK-AHN-KAHR). The Path of Total Awareness; the key to success in unfolding all spiritual powers; the Ancient Science of Soul Travel.

HU (HYOO OR HOO). The secret name for God; the Spirit Current, the prime mover, and the first impulse that came from the Deity; and also the first cause of motion, color, and form.

LIGHT OF GOD. The reflection of the atoms moving in space, as the ECK, the manifestation of the SUGMAD in the lower worlds, flows from the SUGMAD into the lower worlds and then returns.

LIVING ECK MASTER. The Vi-Guru, the Godman; the ECK personified, the true and competent Master who works for the freedom of all Souls, leading them out of the lower planes of existence and beyond into Self-Realization.

MAHANTA. A state of God Consciousness which is beyond the titles given in religions which designate states of consciousness; the highest of all states of consciousness.

PAUL TWITCHELL. The 971st Living ECK Master, 1965-1971.

SOUL. That which has no form, no movement, no location in the worlds of time and space, but has the ability to know, see, hear, and perceive; that is, has perception and the ability to assume or claim a position in the physical or the spiritual worlds; the creative center of man. Atma is another name for Soul.

SOUL TRAVEL. Projection of the inner consciousness, which travels the lower states until It ascends into the ecstatic states; achieved through a series of spiritual exercises known only to the followers of Eckankar.

SOUND OF GOD. Audible Life Current.

SPIRIT. The sustaining power of the SUGMAD; the ECK.

THE SPIRITUAL NOTEBOOK. The title of a book written by Paul Twitchell.

SHARIYAT-KI-SUGMAD (SHAR-REE-AHT-KEE-SOOG-MAHD). Way of the Eternal; the holy scriptures of ECK.

SUGMAD (SOOG-MAHD). The Formless, All-embracing, Impersonal, Infinite; GOD.

ECKANKAR Presents a Spiritual Study Course: *Soul Travel—The Illuminated Way*

People want to know the secrets of life and death. In response to this need Paul Twitchell, the modern-day founder of Eckankar, brought to light the Spiritual Exercises of ECK—which offer a direct way to God.

Those who are ready to begin a study of Eckankar can receive special monthly discourses which give clear, simple instructions for these exercises. The first twelve-month series is called *Soul Travel—The Illuminated Way*. Mailed each month, the discourses are designed to lead the individual to the Light and Sound of God.

The techniques in these discourses, when practiced twenty minutes a day, are likely to prove survival beyond death. Many have used them as a direct route to Self-Realization, where one learns his mission in life. The next stage, God Consciousness, is the joyful state wherein Soul becomes the spiritual traveler, an agent for God. The underlying principle one learns then is this: "Soul exists because God loves It."

Discourses include these titles, among others: "The Universality of Soul Travel," "The Illuminated Way by Direct Projection," and "The Spiritual Cities of This World." These can be studied at home or with fellow students in a local Eckankar class—look in the phone book under Eckankar, or write us for classes in your area.

For more information on how to receive *Soul Travel—The Illuminated Way* and Eckankar classes in your area, use the coupon at the back of this book, or write:

ECKANKAR
P.O. Box 27300
Minneapolis, MN 55427 U.S.A.

Introductory Books on ECKANKAR
The Ancient Science of Soul Travel

The Wind of Change, Sri Harold Klemp

What are the hidden spiritual reasons behind every event in your life? With stories drawn from his own life-long training, Eckankar's spiritual leader shows you how to use the power of Spirit to discover those reasons. Follow him from the Wisconsin farm of his youth, to a military base in Japan; from a job in Texas, into the realms beyond, as he shares the secrets of Eckankar.

In My Soul I Am Free, Brad Steiger

Here is the incredible life story of Paul Twitchell—prophet, healer, Soul Traveler—whose spiritual exercises have helped thousands to contact the Light and Sound of God. Brad Steiger lets the famed ECK Master tell you in his own words about Soul Travel, healing in the Soul body, the role of dreams and sleep, and more. Includes a spiritual exercise called "The Easy Way."

ECKANKAR—The Key to Secret Worlds,
Paul Twitchell

Paul Twitchell, modern-day founder of Eckankar, gives you the basics of this ancient teaching. Includes six specific Soul Travel exercises to see the Light and hear the Sound of God, plus case histories of Soul Travel. Learn to recognize yourself as Soul—and journey into the heavens of the Far Country.

The Tiger's Fang, Paul Twitchell

Paul Twitchell's teacher, Rebazar Tarzs, takes him on a journey through vast worlds of Light and Sound, to sit at the feet of the spiritual Masters. Their conversations bring out the secret of how to draw closer to God—and awaken Soul to Its spiritual destiny. Many have used this book, with its vivid descriptions of heavenly worlds and citizens, to begin their own spiritual adventures.

For more free information about the books and teachings of ECKANKAR, please write: **ECKANKAR, P.O. Box 27300, Minneapolis, MN 55427 U.S.A.**

Or look under ECKANKAR in your local phone book for an ECKANKAR center near you.

For Free Information on ECKANKAR...

☐ Yes, I want free information on Eckankar. Please send me brochures on the Eckankar books and on the twelve-month study series, *Soul Travel—The Illuminated Way.*

☐ I would like information on the nearest Eckankar discussion or study group in my area.

Please type or print clearly   941

Name _____

Street _____

City _____ State/Prov. _____

Zip/Postal Code _____ Country _____

(Our policy: Your name and address are held in strict confidence—we do not rent or sell our mailing lists. Nor will we send anyone to call on you.)

ECKANKAR
P.O. Box 27300
Minneapolis, MN 55427
U.S.A.